ENTER the
STORY

ENTER the
STORY

Biblical Metaphors for Our Lives

Fran Ferder

ORBIS BOOKS

Maryknoll, New York 10545

Founded in 1970, Orbis Books endeavors to publish works that enlighten the mind, nourish the spirit, and challenge the conscience. The publishing arm of the Maryknoll Fathers & Brothers, Orbis seeks to explore the global dimensions of the Christian faith and mission, to invite dialogue with diverse cultures and religious traditions, and to serve the cause of reconciliation and peace. The books published reflect the views of their authors and do not represent the official position of the Maryknoll Society. To learn more about Maryknoll and Orbis Books, please visit our website at www.maryknollsociety.org.

Library of Congress Cataloging-in-Publication Data

Ferder, Fran.
    Enter the story : biblical metaphors for our lives / Fran Ferder.
      p. cm.
    ISBN 978-1-57075-885-0 (pbk.)
    1. Bible stories, English—N.T. 2. Metaphor in the Bible. I. Title.
    BS2400.F47 2010
    225.6'6—dc22

                                                        2010009728

For Nathan Jacob Ferder
November 18, 1977–April 12, 2009

Do not neglect to show hospitality to visitors,
For thereby some have entertained
Angels unawares. (Hb 13:2)

Nathan, my loving and insightful nephew,
visited us for thirty-one years
before succumbing to the effects of muscular dystrophy
on Easter Sunday morning, 2009.
He remains an angel in our midst.

Contents

Preface

Our lives unfold in stories. Perhaps the bible has captivated us for such a long time because it is filled with stories—stories that so transcend time and space that they can happen to any of us, any time. They are vivid, colorful stories with which we can identify—being born, being lost, being fed. They are stories of healing and learning, suffering and dying. They are stories that move us, challenge us, and evoke recognition in our hearts.

Who among us cannot feel the spray of the waves as they crash over the boat during the storm on the lake (Lk 22:23–25) or smell the scent of the ointment or of the woman herself as she dries the feet of Jesus with her hair (Jn 12:3)? We know the thirst-quenching refreshment of a cool drink of water on a hot day, and the deeper thirst that never goes away. We are familiar with dinner parties and wedding feasts, arguments along the way, and the gut-ripping fear of those who wield the sword, whether over our bodies or over our convictions of conscience.

But for anyone who takes this library of stories as a guide for living, the scriptures that we call *sacred* draw us in, inviting us to spend time, entering them deeply enough to be transformed.

THE PURPOSE AND SCOPE OF THIS BOOK

This book assumes that the central stories found in the sacred writings are alive. They happen again and again, much like a great unfinished symphony, in the lives of the people who look to scripture for inspiration. Many biblical stories are *metaphors*—creative accounts about those who first encountered Jesus that point to the same dramas, great and small, that happen in the lives of believers today, every day.

But too often we approach the biblical stories as past events—tragedies and miracles that happened to someone else so far back in history that it can be easier to read *about them* than enter *into them*. We know of a single annunciation, one man's wilderness experience, and the ancient crucifixion of a Nazarene named Jesus. But right now, in this moment, a woman is troubled by an unexpected pregnancy. A man ponders lonely choices in his search to be faithful. An innocent one suffers and dies in the face of injustice. Each of us faces the circumstances of our life at various levels. But for the serious Christian, every one of life's happenings carries within it a call—an opportunity to remember its dynamic connection to a larger story, and a quiet invitation to enter the mystery of our own life with greater consciousness. This means sitting in quiet contemplation, holding the scriptures in one hand and a journal of the happenings of our everyday life in the other. Do the choices that I am making today make love more present in the world? Where do I need healing? How does my behavior need to change in order to support the growth and health of my relationships? Where is gospel love not being felt in my closest relationships, my neighborhood, my church, my world? What annunciation would I have to say yes to? What cross would I have to climb to make love more palpable?

The alternative, of course, is allowing our days to pass, one after the other, seeing no greater meaning in them than the passage of time. We are born. We age. We die. We might find some limited inspiration in the biblical message, but it can easily remain outside of us, disconnected from the narrative of our own lives. Living in faith involves making connections, feeling the relationship between our lives and those of the biblical characters who have gone before us. We all encounter strangers who change us. We are surprised by everyday angels. We travel to visit a beloved relative and come home having felt new life. We carry crosses. We eat with sinners—and they graciously eat with us. This book is an attempt to help ordinary believers read the gospels with greater expectation, hoping to catch a glimpse of how the everyday, seemingly insignificant events of their lives are part of the great mystery of holy stories that were told in the beginning and continue to take shape in our own times.

CHRISTIAN FEASTS AS OUR STORIES

Many of the memorable stories found in scripture are singled out as particularly significant events, and honored as *feast days* or *holy days* in the Christian tradition. But celebrating these feast days and holy days goes beyond commemorating someone else's story. They remind us of our own.

Although the Hebrew and Christian scriptures are like different threads in a many-textured fabric, this book focuses on significant events found in the Christian scriptures, in particular, the gospels. Where deemed helpful, the relationship between the gospel story and its Hebrew context will be explored. But this is primarily a book about significant events, or feasts, in the great Christian story, and the way in which they continue to unfold in everyday human life. They are old stories and new stories. They are unfinished stories. They are our stories.

Acknowledgments

Scripture came alive for me in the late 1960s when I studied under the late biblical scholar and Semitic language expert Father Philip Roets, STL, SSL. As one of the scholars who helped translate the Dead Sea Scrolls, Philip Roets had the ability to hold the attention of an auditorium full of students for an entire weekend course as he translated scripture from the original languages. I will be always indebted to him for his powerful insights and his encouragement to continue my studies.

I am grateful as well to Joan Delaplane, OP; Benedict Viviano, OP; Leslie Hoppe, OFM; Donald Goergin, OP; and Donald Senior, CP; each profoundly influenced my love of scripture during my years of study at Aquinas Institute of Theology. There have been many other scholars and theologians whose writings I have devoured over the years, among them Eugene C. Kennedy; the late Raymond E. Brown, SS; and Elizabeth A. Johnson, CSJ.

My graduate students at Seattle University in the School of Theology and Ministry and those who have participated in workshops I have conducted over the years have helped fine-tune my convictions, influence my vision, and encourage my writing. The Los Angeles Religious Education Congress and many other national and international conference attendees have been a source of inspiration to me for more than twenty-five years. I especially want to thank the participants of the annual Retreat for Women held at San Damiano Retreat House in Danville, California, for the past several summers for their persistent encouragement to "keep writing."

Many religious congregations have graciously invited me to give presentations for their members. Sharing ministry with these vibrant and committed women and men is always a privilege. I want to thank particularly the Sisters of Providence of the Pacific Northwest, including their province in the Philippines; the Holy Cross Sisters, including their province in Bangladesh; the Maryknoll Community; the Franciscan Friars of Santa Barbara, California; and the Carmelite Sisters in Washington and Oregon. Special, singular thanks to the Sisters of Providence at St. Joseph Residence in Seattle for your gracious hospitality and friendship over the years.

To Voice of the Faithful, Call to Action, Call to Action of Western Washington, The Faith Trust Institute, and so many other groups of committed individuals who challenge our world and faith communities to a clearer witness of gospel values, thank you for your commitment and your ongoing support.

To my family and friends, thank you for your ever-present love and support. You give me energy and hope, wonderful meals, and a "home away from home" whenever I need it.

To my Franciscan Community, the Franciscan Sisters of Perpetual Adoration (FSPA): The writing sabbatical you so generously provided gave me the gift of time I needed to research and write this book. I am grateful to you for so much more than that—especially for being one of the most open and affirming communities I have known. I am humbled and proud to be part of you (us). Thank you for your ever present affirmation.

To Michael Leach, my publisher and editor at Orbis Books: Thank you for your trust, for your encouragement, for your advice and ideas, for the lunches at Congress, and for making me laugh when it was most needed. You have been more than patient with this process.

Last, but certainly not least, to John Heagle, my colleague and close friend of more than thirty years: Thank you for all of the times we have shared ministry, prayed, cried, and laughed—and for always being there for me. Our shared vision of the gospels is in these pages.

ENTER the STORY

Chapter 1

Christian Feasts as Metaphors

The Deeper Significance of Gospel Stories

An angel visits a young girl and tells her she will bear the son of God. An entire host of heavenly beings announce the child's birth to shepherds in the night. An ordinary jug of water becomes fine wine. A blind man begins to see, and a silent one finds his voice. A little girl awakens from the dead. A rotting corpse walks out of a tomb. A few loaves of bread and a little fish feed everyone who is hungry. A stranger on the road makes the hearts of fearful people burn with passion again. So did things in the bible really happen this way? From the perspective of historical fact, probably not. From the perspective of faith, absolutely.

BIBLICAL STORY AS MYTH

In the collection of inspired books called the bible there are many kinds of literature, "including poetry, drama, history, and fiction." The late pontifical biblical scholar Raymond E. Brown also notes that the biblical library includes many stories that lie somewhere between history and fiction, in that they are "imaginative retellings"[1]—stories that may contain a core of historical fact but have been further developed to transmit a great spiritual conviction. For example, that a man named Jesus of Nazareth was born provides the core historical fact of the nativity stories, but the

1

details surrounding his birth are "imaginative retellings." The
Roman Catholic Pontifical Biblical Commission issued its "Instruction on the Historicity of the Gospels" in 1964 to assist
Catholics, and other Christians, in navigating these creative biblical waters with greater understanding.[2] The commission understood that there was a difference between penning a biography and writing a gospel.

The gospel writers had a more important mission than pre-
senting their hearers with chronological historical data. They
wrote to inspire belief in the Jesus, "which we have seen with our
eyes, which we have looked upon and touched with our hands"
(1 Jn 1:1). To accomplish this they relied on a process that was
common in their day: they remembered what they had heard
about the historical Jesus and his followers, and they interpreted
it according to the needs of their differing audiences. Drawing
from Hebrew literature for support, they created sacred stories
to convey the significance of Jesus' life, death, and rising. While
some biblical material conforms to records of history, much of it
comes to us as *imaginative retelling*—as stories of faith, narratives
less significant because they are factually accurate and more significant because they invite us into the powerful world of spiritual meaning.

What does this mean for those of us who are not biblical scholars, but who read the gospels seeking more than literal directives
for living? How can contemporary biblical scholarship deepen
our understanding of the life and ministry of Jesus? Many of the
gospel stories are myths, accounts of Jesus and his followers that
may or may not conform to historical fact as prevailing science
understands it, but are *truer than true* in their transcendent reality. Considering this, we can explore how these sacred writings
travel forward in time, break through the confines of history, and
speak a fresh message to our hearts each day.

Myth comes from the Greek word *mythos*, meaning "story," or
"sacred story." Myth is not an untruth—in fact, myth can be re-
garded as *more than true*, as a belief so profound that it cannot be
bound by time or limited to data.[3] In this sense, myth has its
existence both within and beyond history. Like archetypes, the
great themes found in mythology are so embedded in human

consciousness as to be universal. The creation stories of Genesis, for example, are significant variations on other creation stories developed by even earlier peoples who were in touch with the same profound reality—that there is direction and purpose in our existence. Long before the Genesis accounts of creation took shape, other storytellers told of floods, spirit-animated breath, and first creatures rising out of mud to be a people.[4] The significance of the message in the many creation stories does not lie in material details, like the number of days it took to create the world, but in the larger reality that all of the cosmos has its source in the Great Holy. Stories help make this truth believable to different people of all eras by using images that are familiar to them.

Myth, then, carries its message forward not by passing on literal facts, but by telling stories—stories developed, reinterpreted, and retold again and again. Myth, writes Karen Armstrong, "is not a story told for its own sake. Correctly understood, myth puts us in the correct spiritual or psychological posture for right action, in this world or the next."[5] Joseph Campbell describes myth (mythology) as "poetic expressions of . . . transcendental seeing."[6] Myth entails creative attempts to articulate *more* than can be proven. It does so by stirring our hearts, by touching that deep place of wonder in all of us. If myth works, it slows us down just long enough to feel an inclination toward greater generosity and kindness. It has the power to capture our attention and point us toward holy mystery.

Earlier peoples were entirely comfortable surrounding themselves with myths, or sacred stories about life and death, and they had no need to subject these narratives to tests of historical accuracy. If a sacred story worked, if belief in it enabled them to move about the world with less anxiety and greater meaning, then it held truth.[7] Our earliest ancestors relied on myths to answer their ultimate questions about their origins, their relationships with one another, their destiny, and their deities. The fact that myths from different parts of the world at different times in history contain similar elements has led psychologists and philosophers to conclude that mythic consciousness taps into a vast awareness that transcends usual modes of knowing.

In contemporary times our reliance on the scientific method and rational consciousness has diminished the power of myth to move us to mystery. We live in an age where science often trumps mystery. In fact, sacred mystery, or ultimate meaning, has often become a problem to solve rather than a question to carry. For some, the existence of God is believed only if human beings, understood as God's creatures, can *prove* the existence of such a being with philosophical and scientific inquiry—which is a little like trying to dig a thousand-mile-long ditch with a toothpick. We might move some soil around, but we will never come close to accomplishing the task. A demand to "show me the proof" might verify tangible reality, but it is not a pathway to transcendence.

WHERE MYTH AND METAPHOR MEET

Both myth and metaphor involve storytelling that makes use of imagination, combined with symbolic language to carry us beyond the obvious. If myth is sacred story that holds and protects the deepest beliefs of a people, it is metaphor that helps us recognize the relationship between mythic truth and our own lives. The word *metaphor*, in Greek, means "to transfer." It illuminates a connection between one thing and another. Metaphor carries the truth of something, such as a sacred myth, and transfers the deep meaning within its story to our lives. Metaphor helps keep alive the ancient truths in myth by showing us their possibilities for today.

Many of the vivid and inviting stories of the gospels are timeless metaphors for the events that unfold each day in our lives. The more we enter these stories, the more we know that we too are the recipients of an angel's message, or see the path that the wilderness has traced through our own history. As metaphors, gospel stories direct us beyond the biblical characters and acquaint us with the capacity for holy encounter that each of our lives holds.

Every gospel presents its unique theology through vibrant narratives of women and men standing before sacred mystery.

We can approach them as stories about other people and savor the inspiration they offer us from the shadows of history, or we can understand them as alive, flesh and blood events that mirror the great human themes found in our lives today:

- A young woman ponders the meaning of a surprise pregnancy. She travels to visit her kinswoman, who is also pregnant. Their babies are born, circumcised, dedicated to God. Then their lives unfold in quiet ordinariness for nearly three decades. What significance lies in hidden lives? For them? For me?
- A man, barely thirty, has spent the best years of his youth in a family business. But all the while, some other passion stirs in his blood. His family thinks he is crazy. But he must follow his call. He sets out—his dream his only guide. How can he know if his dream is of God? How can I? How can anyone be sure of a life direction?
- A woman is discouraged as she goes about her daily chores. It is hot. The trip has been tedious. She is tired, and alone— again. Then she meets someone who lifts her hopes. Living water? Can she trust the feeling welling up inside of her? Will she finally find her voice? What about my voice—and the voices of others the globe over who have a thirst too deep for words?
- People gather on a hillside. They are hungry—hungry for food, hungry for hope, hungry for love. Will this place feed them? What will nourish any of us? Where am I looking for nurturance?
- A mother watches and waits as her child dies. There is nothing she can do to save him from this cross, though she would gladly climb it and hang there herself if she could. What now? How do I deal with the death of my child? What do I do with grief and loss as searing as this? Will the pain ever diminish?

These are not only gospel stories about people with names like Mary, Elizabeth, John, and Jesus—or narratives of obscure people like the unnamed woman from Samaria. They are also our stories, yours and mine. They invite us to enter into the drama of birth, life, and death from the inside, reading the events of our lives not as separate happenings devoid of meaning, but as part of the great unfolding story of compassionate love.

Is Miriam of Nazareth the only young woman in history who has given birth to a sacred child? Or are there nearly seven billion of us alive this day, each of us "children of God," heirs of a deity whose spirit overshadowed our birth (Rom 8:16–17)? If all of us are sons and daughters of God, did choirs of angels sing for us when we were born? Have stones been rolled back from the tombs of death for anyone but Lazarus? Dare we hope that we might one day pick up the sleeping mats of our crippled places and walk on our own? Or hear more deeply, see more clearly, speak more fearlessly? Will we ever become so transformed that our faces shine like the sun?

It is in this sense that the gospel stories function as metaphors for the joy and pain, the hope and loss, the hunger and fulfillment of human life today. They assume that the good news (*gospel*) continues to be written with our lives. The annunciation isn't a one-time proclamation. The visitation happened today and will occur again tomorrow. The Transfiguration is taking place now— somewhere, to someone, who struggles to change.

JESUS AND METAPHOR

Like other rabbinic leaders of his day Jesus uses symbolic language when he preaches and teaches. His use of allegory in the parables provides a visual image of his message. The parables of Jesus, in their earliest form, probably represent his actual words, or as close as time and translation will allow us to get to them. "Jesus' parables are radically constitutive of his own distinctive historicity."[8] Even though the parables come to us in different versions, depending on which evangelist is telling the story, the import of these sayings of Jesus cannot be underestimated. Not only do they tell us how Jesus understood and responded to the reign of God, but they provide timeless truths applicable to future situations. In the words of biblical scholar John Dominic Crossan, Jesus "was not crucified for parables but for ways of acting which resulted from the experience of God presented in the parables."[9] "Parable," says Crossan, "is the house of God."[10] Parables make a home for the message of justice. They provide a context for a way of being for the believer. If I understand the meaning of a parable, I will be that much closer to understanding how to act in accord with the reign of God.

When Jesus said that the reign of God was "like a mustard seed" (Mt 13:31), or "like leaven which a woman took and hid in three measures of flour" (Lk 13:21), he was not intending that the imagery be taken literally. The reign of God is not synonymous with a mustard seed, nor does leaven hidden in flour fully describe it. But both images, in part because of their simple earthiness, convey a profound truth about God's way of being in the cosmos, including in human life. Our attention should not focus on the tiny mustard seed, or the measure of flour. Instead, each of these images ought to pull us inward, in contemplative reflection, as well as point us outward as we ponder the truth that each holds. What lies between the seed and tree—the leaven and the loaf? What expansive journey occurs that is like God's dream for the earth when a tiny seed becomes a huge tree? What dramatic growth, like leaven causing dough to rise, takes place in the hearts and minds of the daughters and sons of God when God's way of justice slowly becomes our way of treating one another?

The images used in parable, or in any figurative speech, are not chosen for their exactness but for their evocative quality. The common mustard seed, for example, does not usually grow into a huge tree—more often it is like a large shrub.[11] So, the truth of the parable does not lie in the precision of its parts, but in its ability to teach us something about God's way. Pushing the symbol further, a mustard *shrub*, once it takes hold, reseeds itself and spreads throughout the area in a wild and unpredictable manner. It can become as annoying as a weed as it overgrows its original boundaries. Its ability to take root and to spread evokes an image of the reign of God. God's way of compassion and inclusivity has a way of expanding—often in a manner that irritates those who prefer that God's style of operating in the world would be predictable, and more in their control. But once it takes hold in even one human heart, its nature is to increase, to reach into a community, and to continue to broaden its influence. Its smallness in the beginning is no predictor of its capacity for unstoppable growth. The more any of us practice compassion, the more it becomes familiar, spreading into unsuspecting crevices of our subconscious, alerting us to places where empathy is needed. Like a spiritual knee-jerk response, our feeling for the plight of others becomes automatic. When that happens, the secret of the mustard shrub has been incorporated into our souls. The reign of God has another advocate!

The biblical writers present Jesus as having a keen awareness about the power of suggestion inherent in symbolic story. When the disciples ask him why he addresses the crowds in parables, Jesus knows about the different layers of meaning hidden in stories. He notes the distinction between the genuine disciple, or learner, and "the crowds"—symbolic of those who lack the ability, or the will to deeply internalize the message of the reign of God (Mt 13:11–16). Some biblical commentators suggest that references to parables that hide meaning from all but a privileged few point to the influence of Gnosticism,[12] which gradually crept into later biblical writings. While such Gnostic influence may be present, especially in later Christian writings, it does not negate the fact that Jesus used stories to teach and preach, or that stories contain varying levels of meaning.

A superficial reception of the word will not bring about genuine understanding of how God is present to the world. The true disciple, one who actually gets the message, must be ready to go beneath literal details to deeper spiritual significance. Not everyone can do this. Jesus likens some of the people of his day to those of whom Isaiah spoke:

"You shall indeed hear but never understand,
and you shall indeed see but never perceive.
For this people's heart has grown dull,
and their ears are heavy of hearing,

> *and their eyes they have closed,*
> *lest they should perceive with their eyes,*
> *and hear with their ears,*
> *and understand with their heart,*
> *and turn for me to heal them." (Mt 13:14–15)*

Ears that don't hear. Eyes that are closed. Hearts too dull to understand. The biblical writers suggest that understanding God's reign requires openness, fresh perception, and a passionate heart. In speaking of those who "don't get it," Jesus isn't just referencing the ignorant who lack the capacity to plumb the depths of a parable, or those who have not been given the gift of seeing and hearing the teaching about God's reign. There were others who did not receive his message. Some of them were teachers of the Law.

The tension between Jesus and the religious leaders of his day is well documented in the Christian writings. Some of them resisted new ways of seeing, hearing, and understanding because of their self-righteous arrogance. Many of them would have been intellectually astute and so certain of their own view of God's ways that their eyes, ears, and hearts were closed to the simple yet surprising truth of a more expansive way of understanding the reign of God. They heard and saw only what they themselves defined as truth—a truth they attempted to control. They had lost their sense of wonder. In quoting Isaiah, the evangelists were likely singling out those who had escalated their fight against the Christian message when the first gospels were taking shape. But their words offer a biblical insight about *openness* that is timeless. First articulated in the Hebrew bible, and expressed again by early Christian writers, the repetitive nature of this gradually developing conviction makes it especially noteworthy. Not just a passing notion from the ancients, but a profound belief that deepened and took on flesh over time, *a stance of openness* achieves the status of biblical mandate for all believers—open eyes, open ears, open hearts are among the marks of the follower of Jesus.

Any of us who claims to understand truth in all its fullness will miss any further revelation of the holy. Those who believe that

God speaks only to them have already lost the capacity to hear anyone else. Their ears have indeed grown heavy from listening to their own voices. If my eyes can only recognize my own view of reality, I am blind to all that is seen from vantage points other than mine. Dull hearts are perhaps the saddest of all. They feel no joy, no excitement, and no love. Compassion, the hallmark of the believer, is lost to them.

Perhaps the greatest enemy of truth is too much certainty about it. It is not prostitutes, tax collectors, and sinners—weak-willed and broken human beings—that are the real threats for Jesus. Heavy ears, closed eyes, and dull hearts represent an eloquent image of the real opponents of the gospel. Whether we are fervent individuals or prominent leaders of religious institutions, biblical symbol as strong as this ought to make us nervous—and a little more reluctant to elevate our opinions to the pedestal of irrefutable dogma, much less punish those who see a different reality.

When the shocking impact of such images is minimized, it is easy to turn the heaviness of gospel stories into little more than pious recitations that have minimal capacity to stir our souls and deter us from cruel treatment of one another. What does it *really* mean to have eyes that are closed? What is it that I do not see in such a state? And what about ears that don't hear, or hearts that have lost their capacity to be moved? What do they symbolize?

Has there ever been a time when the suffering of another person did not affect me? In everyday life, if I win an argument, is there any part of me that feels for the person who lost—and wants to reach out? How often do I change the TV channel when the news depicts the tragic plight of others whose lives are remote from mine? Whose story do I block out? Whose pain do I intentionally try to forget? None of us can absorb the sorrow of the whole world, but at some point, and in some situations I need to confront myself with the question God posed to the prophets: "Jeremiah, what do you see?" (Jer 1:11). In Jeremiah's life the signs were painful but there was also promise. He would discover the promise not by avoiding the pain but by turning into it. It is the same for you and me.

WHEN SYMBOLIC LANGUAGE
IS INTERPRETED LITERALLY

When myth and metaphor are literalized their mystery is lost. When any figurative language is interpreted for its own sake, or reduced to the sum of its definable or provable parts, transcendent meaning is erased. Stripped of its spiritual power, it can do little more than distract, entertain, or lull us into a false spiritual security.

Even so, there are many people, including some religious leaders, who find literal certainty appealing. The factual accuracy of the bible is necessary for their faith or at least more comfortable than living with ambiguity. They seek assurance in biblical writings by interpreting this collection of stories literally—a phenomenon sometimes called biblical fundamentalism. While there may be technical differences between the biblical literalist and the fundamentalist, both look to the exact words for truth and are either wary of biblical criticism or reject it completely—the many contradictions within the bible and the complexities inherent in translation notwithstanding. When this happens, the deeper theological meaning of the biblical message is exchanged, often selectively, for a surface understanding that may altogether miss the theological point that the biblical writers are making.

In the Judeo-Christian tradition virtually every biblical story with potential for interpretation has been subjected to literalism—especially those that can be used to support or refute particular ideologies. It is fascinating to see how biblical literalism is often associated with systems of political belief and personal prejudice. One of the most striking examples is the use of the bible to condemn homosexuality—even though translation of the few references to behavior that is presumed to constitute same-sex activity requires suspending information about the actual meaning of the Hebrew words referenced, as well as ignoring the cultural issues of the times. Linguistic gymnastics have been applied to the bible to support everything from slavery, racism, and sexism to war and the death penalty.

Examples of this abound in all faith traditions. In the Muslim world, *jihad* is the Arabic word for battle or struggle. Taken literally, such a word can invite or even mandate the killing of infidels, regarding such bloody slaughter as a holy act, pleasing to Allah. Taken metaphorically, *jihad* refers to the spiritual "warfare" that one might enter into with oneself to eradicate all vices and sharpen perception of Allah's goodness. The difference between literal and metaphorical interpretations of figurative language is astounding—and makes all the difference between living in peace and cooperation on our tenuous planet, or endless war, where some of the children of God kill others of the children of God in the name of the God who created them all.

Fundamentalism tends to intensify in a culture at times of stress and uncertainty. If the world around them is chaotic, and seems without direction, people can find concrete answers in biblical fundamentalism. While this may provide security, it may also take them further and further away from actual faith—a stance of the heart that implies the willingness to suspend the need for ready answers and live in trust.

BIBLICAL FAITH AND MYTH

Most simply put, faith is trust. It is confidence without proof, daily reliance without evidence of special treatment, assurance in the midst of wilderness. Faith, in the first place, is not assent to a set of religious statements or doctrines. Although we may talk about "professing our faith," we do so less by reciting a creed and more by living a life of dependence upon the persistent presence of love and doing our best to make that love present to others. Even the strongest faith has questions, doubts, and times of struggle simply because trusting is hard. It meets obstacles and challenges that try human endurance to the utmost.

Spiritual myth stands in the service of biblical faith, offering images and stories that bring faith alive. True faith does not demand that religious myths be transparent, or explainable—only that they inspire goodness in those who internalize their message. In many ways allowing the meaning in myth to reveal itself requires an act of faith. Because myth does not lend itself to usual ways of interpreting reality, standing before its truths in humble receptivity can take us to the edge of holy mystery. Allowing faith and myth to walk hand in hand does not require the elimination of doubt, but rather the suspension of scientific certainty. Doubt is less an enemy of biblical faith than is the quest for literal certainty. Myth can arouse faith even as faith inspires the quest to delve into the meaning of myth.

Examples of biblical faith abound in the gospels. Always, faith is about trust in God, not agreement with teachings or doctrines. When Jesus witnesses living faith in people, he knows that they are in touch with something beyond mere human attainment, and he appears to stand in awe of it. When a centurion comes asking Jesus to heal his servant, the man's faith tells him that Jesus can do this simply by speaking the word (Mt 8:8). When Jesus hears this, he is amazed and says, "In no one in Israel have I found such faith" (Mt 8:10). For Jesus, faith is first of all a relationship of utter confidence and is all the more surprising here because the centurion is a Gentile official—he was the "other." A foreigner witnesses faith that causes even Jesus to marvel! In the community of disciples we should expect surprises. Those who least fit our categories of belonging can become our teachers. The centurion evokes wonder in Jesus not because he has intricate knowledge of the Law or precise answers to religious questions. Jesus marvels because the centurion has simple, humble faith. He believes. It is the beginning of far-reaching healing—for everyone. The distressed and paralyzed servant is healed. The centurion is relieved of his worry. The followers witness a long-distance miracle—whether of body or spirit is open to interpretation. And Jesus emerges from this event amazed at the far-reaching power of faith in one considered an outsider.

What does one defined as the "other" offer today? Do immigrants desperately attempting to cross the border from one country into another in search of a better life teach us anything about persistence or fairness? Are they modern versions of the relentless woman of the gospels who violates the rules to touch the hem of Jesus' garment and find healing? What about gay and lesbian persons who continue to seek a place at the table in our faith communities, bringing with them their lives of love and service? Are they like the Gentiles who are excluded simply for being different? If the response of Jesus and his early followers is any example, would they not be at the table? Try to imagine what a table would look like today if the behavior and example of Jesus actually determined the guest list. Think of any table—dinner tables, restaurant tables, picnic tables, eucharistic tables. Who would be there and what would be the seating arrangements?

THE POWER OF STORY

In Matthew's gospel there is an interesting interplay among doubt, faith, and metaphor when the disciples of Jesus fail to understand his use of symbolic language:

> *When the disciples reached the other side,*
> *they had forgotten to bring any bread.*
> *Jesus said to them, "Watch out, and beware of the yeast of the*
> *Pharisees and Sadducees."*
> *They said to one another, "It is because we have brought no bread."*
> *And becoming aware of it, Jesus said, "You of little faith,*
> *why are you talking about having no bread?" (Mt 16:5–8)*

Jesus then recalls feeding the people and having baskets with a surplus of food left over—a stern reminder to the disciples to have faith in him. Then, Jesus corrects their failure to interpret the symbolic meaning of his words:

> *"How could you fail to perceive that I was not speaking about bread?*
> *Beware of the yeast of the Pharisees and Sadducees!"*
> *Then they understood that he had not told them to beware of the*
> *yeast of bread,*
> *but of the teaching of the Pharisees and Sadducees. (Mt 16:11–12)*

Being a disciple (learner) requires consistent reminders to look beyond the obvious, to leave the easy, literal interpretations behind and seek the deep-seated meanings in biblical narratives.

The "yeast of the Pharisees" was not about actual yeast, or even bread dough, but about the insidious capacity of words to spread a misleading message about God's reign of compassion and justice. Ironically, the same problem of misunderstanding persists in our times. How often does a literal interpretation of a biblical story about justice become skewed into one that effects injustice? Perhaps Jesus' correction of the disciples is aimed at all of us who would like to settle for the shallow meanings of words and stories, who would like things to be simple.

In this gospel story, where baskets of leftover loaves can still mystify the very disciples who collected them, and symbolic meaning is kneaded into words like yeast, we can feel the slow movement toward biblical faith. It is like bread rising, like seeds taking root, like a woman searching the interior of her house for something she knows is there but can't find yet. Biblical faith is like unfinished corners in our souls that need time—time for nurturance, time for wondering, time for hidden possibilities to find their way to the surface. It can't be rushed, and it most certainly cannot be captured by a creed and recited on Sundays. Collective statements of belief, or creeds, have a place in liturgical ritual, but in everyday life they can never substitute for the sometimes hesitant and troubled trust in the holy that dwells in our hearts. Biblical faith has as many faces as there are love stories, and it prefers wonder over proof.

WHEN STORIES POINT THE WAY

There will be more miracles, more journeys, more prayer—and more stories as Jesus and his disciples, yesterday and today, move toward understanding what it means to bring about God's dream. The journey of faith took the disciples of the first Christian century through the winding road of figurative language where stories point the way less clearly than maps, and signs are posted in the heart. It will be no easier for us. There is no Map Quest for discipleship. The destination toward which we journey is less a place than an experience. We will know we are moving in the right direction if tables along the way are crowded and bewildered waiters collect leftover pieces of bread long into the night. Movement toward the reign of the holy will likely convince us that much of our idiosyncratic certainty about how things should be is baggage best left behind, along with prejudice, violence, and any religious ideal that excludes strangers from joining. All we need to enter the feast is our own hunger, eyes clear enough to see the hunger of those who travel with us—and a keen awareness of those who are missing from the table.

Chapter 2

Annunciation

Sacred Announcements

In the sixth month the angel Gabriel was sent from God
to a city of Galilee named Nazareth, to a virgin
betrothed to a man whose name was Joseph, of the house of David;
and the virgin's name was Mary.
And he came to her and said, "Hail, O favored one,
the Lord is with you!"
But she was greatly troubled at the saying,
and considered in her mind what sort of greeting this might be.
And the angel said to her, "Do not be afraid, Mary,
for you have found favor with God.
And behold, you will conceive in your womb and bear a son,
and you shall call his name Jesus . . .
And Mary said to the angel, "How shall this be,
since I have no husband?"
And the angel said to her, "The Holy Spirit will come upon you,
and the power of the Most High will overshadow you;
therefore the child to be born will be called holy,
the Son of God." (Lk 1:26–31, 34–35)

An angelic birth announcement and a peasant girl set the stage
for Christianity. Yet the powerful symbolism of Luke's annunciation narrative has likely had less influence in the imagination of
most Christians than have the many artistic renditions of the

scene. One of the most frequent subjects in art, the annunciation to Mary is part of the repertoire of all of the great masters. Whether captured in a plaster fresco in a grand cathedral, painted larger than life in the Uffizi Gallery in Florence, or hanging in a worn frame in your family home, the imagery of the annunciation is deeply etched into religious consciousness. Its popularity, with artists and ordinary folks alike, is its ability to give us hope in the face of the impossible—hope in God's abiding presence, hope in our capacity for greatness, hope in the possibility that a loving and holy God would find sufficient favor with us to invite our participation in birthing a new creation.

IMAGINING THE ANNUNCIATION

The early representations of the annunciation in art are ornate. Appearing in the late Middle Ages, each portrays the artist's particular image of how it might have taken place. Mary can be seen kneeling, sitting, or standing, reading or praying. She is blond or brunette, veiled or bare headed and clothed in the garments of the artist's time in history. She is almost always demure in manner. Her features usually appear Caucasian in medieval and Renaissance art, and the setting is typically grand, if not opulent—hardly a historically accurate portrayal of a Jewish peasant girl.

More modern renditions of the annunciation portray Mary with Asian, African, or Indian features, often dependent on the ethnicity of the artist. Chinese artist He Qi painted a decidedly Asian Mary in a bright purple dress, playing a reed instrument, while an Asian-featured Gabriel looks on. Prestigious contemporary American artist John Collier paints a pony-tailed, teenaged Mary on a porch in suburbia.[1] In these works Mary has lost her Jewish features altogether, along with any hint of her social and historical setting. The great variety and even inconsistency in these creative works do not prevent inspiration, but rather enhance it. Art is not intended to be interpreted literally. Its meaning is revealed in layers, and different viewers see different things in the same artistic work. What inspires me might not appeal to you. The painting that calls forth your tears might not evoke mine. An inspirational aspect of sacred art is its ability to highlight human diversity—we are all in the painting. Whatever the color of our hair or skin, our ethnicity or our age, Mary represents *us*. Gabriel's message to Mary is also given to each of us: The spirit of the holy shadows over you. You carry God!

A simple review of the annunciation in art reveals something all artists know: Paintings are *inside them* before they find their way onto canvas. They represent a poetic interaction of biblical story, visual imagery, and psychological projection from within the imagination of each artist. None of us would gaze upon a painting of the annunciation and claim it to be untrue because it does not match the literal words of the story or the historical reality of the setting it represents. Have you ever turned away from a painting of the annunciation because Mary is portrayed as Caucasian—a clear contradiction of her historical reality? Have you found inspiration in the Black Madonna? We expect creative interpretation in art, even though it might not conform to our subconscious stereotypes. It is the interpretation, by the artist, not the exactness of its representation that has the greatest capacity to move our hearts. Mary of Nazareth is the archetype of goodness inside every artist. She makes her home within any of us who can imagine the face of love.

The gospels are art in written form. Matthew, Mark, Luke, and John are dancers with a pen, painters not of picture but of story. They start where every artist starts—with what is *inside them:* passion, conviction, vision, *inspiration*. They write because they must—because an inexplicable force inspires them to give outward expression to what they have come to know on the inside. All four evangelists write about the same events, not because the story has not been told adequately, but because something new stirs within each of them. Prompted by an inner Spirit, they are compelled to "write the vision; make it plain upon tablets so he may run who reads it" (Hb 2:2). In other words, write the story as you understand it. Make it plain for the readers of your time. Be creative. Play with the scene and make it come alive in a new way. Those who read it will "run with it," finding inspiration not in its conformity to historical data but in its capacity to touch their hearts and stir their faith. The author of

Luke-Acts acknowledges that "many have undertaken to compile a narrative of the things which have been accomplished among us" (Lk 1:1), but Luke still undertakes the same creative task of writing a gospel. He knows the same thing that every great painter knows. Some things cannot be expressed enough. One artist cannot capture all that a great story holds. The God who inspires him knows the same thing.

THE ANNUNCIATION IN THE GOSPELS

Matthew and Luke both mention the annunciation, but only Luke presents an actual account of it. Luke actually has two annunciations—the first to Zachariah of the birth of John the Baptist, and the second to Mary of the birth of Jesus. From the perspective of Lucan theology, both annunciations must be understood together. According to biblical scholar Eugene LaVerdiere, Luke uses a series of contrasts in his two annunciation stories to introduce his fundamental christological statement that Jesus is the Son of God.[2] Both annunciation stories are part of the nativity narratives created by Matthew and Luke to elicit faith in Jesus, not only for their first-century hearers, but for future Christians. These stories represent biblical myth at its most compelling, *imaginative retellings* important not for the accuracy of their historical fact, but for the depth of their christological truth—most simply put, that God is with us in Jesus.

MARY

Beyond and beneath christological statements lie stories of simple people whose lives we intuitively recognize. In particular, there is Mary. "As the readers identify with Mary, her story becomes their story."[3] Mary of Nazareth was a real person, a Jewish peasant girl, little more than a teenager when she gave birth to her first child. Hers is "a prophetic vocation story of a Jewish girl and her God, set within the traditions of her people struggling for freedom."[4] In Luke's evocative narrative we are told that she lives in Nazareth, that she is a virgin (or maiden of marriageable age),[5] that she is betrothed to a man named Joseph, and that her name is Mary. Drawing from Hebrew sources, Luke's ordering of words in this descriptive introduction situates the child to be born within the context of what first-century Christians had come to believe about him—that he was the son of God.

Yet, looking at the narrative itself, the order of these introductory statements is telling. We learn where Mary lives, her status in the patriarchal world of her time, the name of her betrothed, and *his* ancestral heritage before we are even given her name. Nazareth. Virgin. Betrothed. Joseph. House of David. Mary. It is her story and God's, yet she is the last to be identified. We know from the narrative that she is a virgin before we are introduced to her as a person with a name. Luke's theological intent aside, the visual and auditory impact of his ordering rightly describes the significance of a woman of her times. She is last. Her virginity is first. Her marriageable state is a more important descriptive than her name.

"A virgin betrothed to a man named Joseph." Mary is labeled before she is named. How many times have you been in a group that referred to others as "welfare mothers," "illegals," or "radical feminists"? How often have you singled out people by a characteristic, putting them into a category, forgetting that they have names—and feelings? Has anyone ever pigeonholed you, perhaps without you knowing it? Anytime people's individual identity becomes subservient to their cultural, physical, or ethnic circumstances, their individual story is lost. Thinking of Mary, "the unwed mother," is a stark reminder that labeling people not only hurts them, it misses the larger truth of their lives. Mary of Nazareth would be the first to understand the feeling of having identity and worth dependent on something other than personhood. In this sense Mary stands as a beacon of hope for all disenfranchised people, women and men reduced to a category or a commodity while individually remaining nameless. Like many good people who offer up quiet acts of service every day, the young woman who responded to the invitation inherent in the incarnation was a social nobody in her time. She is the heroine in the film *Precious*, reminding us that we all have a story and a name.

Mary of Nazareth. It was a name so common that she could have been confused with any one of a number of Marys from the same region. The name appears frequently enough in the gospels that it can be a challenge to identify the exact person being referenced. Perhaps this is part of the deeper meaning of Mary. She is familiar, ordinary, our generous next-door neighbor, the kind mother of one of our children's friends. She is truly each of us who seeks to be a disciple. She is Maria and Maureen, Mara and Marjorie. She is Michael and Paul, Jose and Jorge. She is every person who doesn't stick out in a crowd, who works hard, who goes about her life with a heart open to meet unexpected angels and ponder their message. She is you. She is every woman and man whose birth of goodness makes the world a gentler place.

Nazareth, Mary's hometown, was a village of poverty and oppression. A young girl growing up here had little opportunity to rise out of a situation of illiteracy, dawn-to-dusk work, and ongoing childbearing. Her primary value, as a female child, is her physical virginity, rendering her acceptable for marriage. Were she to lose her virginity in any manner prior to the marriage ceremony that completes her betrothal, her worth and her future would be severely jeopardized. Her anguish would have been very real had her virginity been compromised in any way—a reality that is easily lost in the poetic narrative. Ironically, Matthew highlights this as Joseph's dilemma rather than Mary's (Mt 1:18–19). Her potential calamity is given only passing reference in Luke's verses. His purpose is not to highlight the terrible plight of a pregnant young girl who is supposed to be virginal, but to move quickly to Jesus and his divine status as the son of God. Even inspired evangelists are influenced by their culture and have limitations of insight.

Still, it is this "last one," the least in importance in the patriarchal order, with only her virginity to offer, who is chosen to play the most significant of roles in the history of God's far-reaching reign of compassion. In human ordering prized characteristics such as skin color, physical beauty, youth, and social position give us value. In God's way of ordering the last shall be first. This message is conveyed loudly at the outset of Jesus' life. He inherits from his Jewish parents the calluses of the poor and the insignificance of one born in such a place as Nazareth—and a teenaged peasant mother favored by a God who accords places of honor to the downtrodden.[6]

MARY'S VIRGINITY

Much has been written about Mary's virginity.[7] The Catholic Church has placed more significance on it than did the patriarchal society in which she lived, declaring her a virgin before, during, and after the conception and birth of Jesus. This pronouncement, which is part of church doctrine, elevates the expected virginity of a young woman before marriage and expands it—a notion that some consider foreign to Mary's Jewish heritage. While there is agreement among the evangelists that a young woman named Mary of Nazareth was the actual mother of Jesus, the meaning of her virginity prior to his birth continues to be explored. Some argue that we cannot look to the scriptures for proof of Mary's initial physical virginity, much less a virginity that remained intact through childbirth and marriage. Aside from the absence of a single biblical reference to Mary's *perpetual* virginity, the doctrine might raise other troubling questions.

Did a negative theology of sexuality occasion the perceived need for Mary to remain a virgin all her life? Would it compromise her goodness and purity in any way had she and Joseph, her husband, been physically passionate lovers? Does proclamation of Mary's perpetual virginity denigrate the sacredness of sexual lovemaking in marriage? Does the suggestion that Mary underwent childbirth while remaining virginal demean women who pant and sweat, stretch and tear every day to bring forth newborn sons and daughters of God? Would the very God who fashioned all of the processes by which life originates, including sexual loving, sidestep this very creation to accomplish incarnation? Incarnation—God with us—like us in everything, with us in tender and wild loving, with us in uniting ovum and sperm, with us on delivery room altars where blood and water mingle and the shrill cry of the newborn announces incarnation once again? Can a literal interpretation of perpetual virginity place Mary of Nazareth outside of the very human condition that incarnation proclaims? God is with us. The word becomes flesh. The holy does not escape any aspect of humanness. To be a virgin, in the strictly physical sense, implies the absence of sexual experience—as in the case of a female whose vagina has never been entered. But physical virginity alone does not make a person great, or a great person greater. An intact hymen (something of a myth in itself) does not equal an intact self. Attaching lofty spiritual significance to such a state does not tell us anything about the whole person—how she thinks, what she feels, or who she loves. It is silent about the depth of her spirituality. There are mean-spirited virgins, selfish virgins, angry virgins—virgins who make the world a harsher place, not at all a welcoming space for the holy.

Can placing an exaggerated spiritual value on physical virginity deal another insult to those women and men who have been sexually violated? When physical virginity is held up as the highest gift one can give to God, or to one's spouse, where does such emphasis leave rape victims and others whose virginity has been taken from them by force or manipulation? What of those whose sexual choices, whether healthy or unhealthy, have compromised their physical virginity but left their hearts eager for healing and open to loving? How can Mary of Nazareth be a spiritual model for them? If a virginal womb, sealed forever, is a requirement for incarnation, how does the word become incarnate now through the tired and sometimes abused bodies of those who also hear an angel sent by God inviting them to bear the holy into the world of today?

Some have argued that making a young woman's physical virginity a requirement for marriage is associated with male control over women's bodies—and with patriarchal governance in a society or an institution. It existed in Mary's time in history and still exists today in all parts of the globe. Honor killings, sometimes barbaric, take place routinely in our world, almost always against women for some perceived sexual indiscretion. A simple

Internet review reveals both the frequency and horror of what some are calling gendercide—the murder of young girls and women by male relatives for something as simple as having an unknown number programmed into a cell phone. Sex before marriage merits the most brutal of punishments, including death in some cultures. Is elevating Mary's initial bodily virginity prior to the conception of her firstborn child to a lifetime of physical virginity creating unwitting complicity in the harsh punishments inflicted on those who fail to live up to the sexual standards of their patriarchal cultures?

It is important that church doctrine on Mary's perpetual virginity not place her on that psychic pedestal where female sexuality is either denied by those who detest it or exalted by those whose ultimate fantasy is the woman who is forever virginal, even after childbirth.

MARY'S VIRGINITY AS METAPHOR

Many authors have understood Mary's virginity as a metaphor for her readiness to face whatever is asked of her.[8] True virginity is "an attitude of being open and available to divine mystery, to the voice and power of the spirit in us."[9] From a psychological perspective, virginity can be understood as an uncluttered mind, clarity of perception, an unfettered spirit. The virginal individual is one who does not take her identity from anyone else. She has given over her power to no one. She refuses to be used, either sexually or in any other way. She knows who she is because she has searched her own heart and found there a quiet center. The true virgin, with or without sexual experience, is one whose *being* is intact. She is uncompromising in her integrity. Her purity lies in her heart, and her experiences, by whatever name, make their home in a self that has chosen its life and offered its own fiat to whatever parts of it are beyond choosing.

We can continue to refer to the "virgin Mary," understanding that her virginity holds a mystery that goes beyond the physical state. We can also think of her as Mary, or Miriam, of Nazareth (Maryan in Islam), mother of Jesus, co-parent with Joseph—a

Jewish peasant girl of extraordinary strength and an uncommon ability to read in the bewildering signs of her own life a call from a compassionate and ever present God.[10] For some, Mary of Nazareth is a mother, a sexual partner, and more important, a strong woman who took responsibility for her life in the midst of the most difficult of circumstances. Inviting Mary of Nazareth to stand as symbol of holiness for all women, indeed all people, requires that we think beyond a title of perpetual virginity and allow her to have her body—with all of its wondrous powers. Stripping all hints of sexual and sensual reality from Mary of Nazareth does the mystery of the incarnation no favors.

FAVORED

"Hail, O favored one, the Lord is with you!" (Lk 1:28). This is a standard angel greeting, uttered to others before her. We are told that Mary was greatly troubled *(dietarachthe)* and "puzzled over in her mind" what such a greeting might mean (Lk 1:29). She is presented as a young woman of deep thought, as someone who uses her mind to try to figure out things that perplex her. The Greek word *diatarasso* (puzzled) implies an inner struggle, a serious process of sorting out predicaments for which there are no easy explanations. This is our first introduction to Luke's Mary of Nazareth. A real person, she feels and she thinks. She claims time for her own process of inner discernment. Like any of us, she can become anxious in the face of the unexpected. But in the midst of her turmoil, she comes to know that God's *favor* is present. The abiding presence of a God of love that bursts into confused places of our lives when least expected, but most needed, is there.

While some commentators have suggested that Mary somehow earned God's favor because of her unusually pious life up to that point, the truth is that there are no sources that tell us anything about her personality or behavior as a young girl. Luke presents Mary as *favored* not because of anything she has done but simply because the God who is Love is with her. That is the way of grace. It is gift, freely given. It is love, lavishly poured out over a son or daughter even in the worst of times. Such favor from this extravagant God is extended to unmarried pregnant teenagers today as fully as it was to the first unwed mother of the gospels.

Being favored, or graced, does not spare us from turmoil. Like anyone receiving news of an unexpected pregnancy, there is no privileged way for Mary to prepare for the birth that was to come. A sober realism had likely conditioned the hopes of this young Mary—simple hopes that her husband would be kind and care for her well, that she would survive childbirth as many times as she would endure it, that her children would be healthy, that there would be enough food. Hers would have been unadorned dreams, those that characterize hard-working people everywhere—dreams of less harshness, more relief in everyday life, no real expectation of being lifted out of their condition, and no pregnancy prior to marriage. Mary's life prefigures mothers in modern-day Afghanistan and Pakistan whose hope is directed to others: "We don't want our babies to die, and we want our children to go to school."[11]

The sign of God's favor is not lavish success, great fortune, or freedom from pain. The word for favor in Greek (charis) means "grace" or "blessing." Every event of our lives is itself a gift that holds the promise of blessing. Who would think of an unplanned pregnancy as a gift? How could an illness, a divorce, a lost job ever turn into blessing? The word itself holds the key. Favor (charis) also means "gratitude" or "thanks." How we receive the unexpected helps to shape its outcome in our lives. A loss tearfully accepted, a surprise embraced, stunning news eventually given a hearing—all the things that happen to us, or around us, things we are ill-prepared to face, can eventually bless and grace our lives if we make space for them. Like Mary, we ask, "How shall this be?" It is as much a query about outcomes as about causes. How will I deal with this? How will it all turn out? What will become of the person I love? Where do I turn now? Asking the questions and puzzling over possibilities, as Mary did, are part of making space for the unexpected. They are signs, at least, that we are not rejecting the unavoidable turn of events that has been thrust into our lives. An attitude of receptivity to life is the beginning of grace. It opens up an inner home for those things that we might ordinarily resist. *Charis* helps us cry and talk, pray and wait. It softens us. It eases the landing place. We know grace has visited us when gratitude replaces bitterness, and compassion warms the colder places of our hearts.

DO NOT BE AFRAID, MARY

"Do not be afraid." These words, which often accompany angelic greetings in the scriptures, reveal more than figurative references to similar biblical announcements. The narrative suggests empathic tenderness on the part of God's spokesperson toward the young maiden who was stunned by the implications of being favored by God. Do not be afraid. The Greek word *(phobeo)* actually means "terror"—etymologically, "to shake with fear."[12] It would have been terrifying indeed to find oneself pregnant outside of patriarchal sanction. "The terror of her situation should be allowed once again to fertilize the Christian imagination, which has tended to 'wrap Mary in an aura of romantic joy' at finding herself pregnant."[13] Romantic joy was not the response of this young peasant woman in discovering her pregnancy. The angel's words, formulaic as they were, were perceptive. A young woman in Mary's time, inexperienced with pregnancy—and no "drugstore test" to help confirm it, would have experienced mounting fear as one month followed another without menstruation. It would have been common for an uneducated young woman to be certain of her pregnancy only after she began to show or to feel fetal movement. Once confirmed, there is little time for explanations—only shame, shunning, and "perhaps a life of begging, perhaps even death loomed before her."[14]

Do not be afraid. If anyone needs to hear those words, and find in them a way to cope with her dilemma, it is a betrothed maiden, pregnant too soon in a patriarchal world. A life of fear is not what God has in mind for Mary, or for any of us. A pregnancy that violates patriarchal social norms should not be a source of terror. God's comfort surrounds the woman who is victimized and terrorized by controlling and unjust social structures. In such situations each one of us who claims to mirror the presence of the compassionate God in the world is called upon to be an angel—a messenger offering comfort and care, announcing God's favor once again.

Do not be afraid. These reassuring words are often spoken in scripture to those who are panic stricken in response to a surprising event or horrifying situation: "Do not fear; only believe, and she shall be well," Jesus says to the ruler who fears for his sick little daughter's life (Lk 8:50). "Fear not, therefore; you are of more value than many sparrows," he reminds the Twelve in a long instruction about their ministry (Mt 10:31). And when a fierce storm comes up and threatens their boat, the alarmed disciples hear his comforting words coming to them across the churning waves: "It is I; do not be afraid" (Jn 6:20).

Do not be afraid. It is the voice of God within her, comforting Mary from the start. Does she repeat the message over and over in her heart to remind herself, as you and I sometimes do? *Don't be afraid. Don't be afraid. Don't be afraid.* Fear is a response to perceived danger. It is our imagination of the future, a future that rarely turns out exactly as we have anticipated it. We fear for our health, for our reputation, for our children, long before anything bad happens. We panic when our teenagers stay out too late and dread waiting for the results of a medical test. We fear for our loved ones, our country, and our world. Whatever the source of our terror, the God who sent Gabriel to ease the fear of a young maiden in an out-of-the-way village seeks also to move into the places of our distress with words of consolation: *Do not be afraid.* The words do not take away the source of the fear. They do not back up history on an ill-timed pregnancy or prevent the death of a loved one. Accidents will happen, and soldiers will go to war. To release fear does not mean that things will be different, or that all will be well.

Social-change and anti-violence activist Vincent G. Harding, in an open letter written to President Obama urging him not to be afraid, admits his own past fears:

> But that is not easily said, for it brings to my mind those other dangerous and demanding nights when my late wife and I marched into the terror-filled Southern darkness along

with so many of your Freedom Movement ancestors, loudly singing, "We are not afraid." And even as we sang our knees were trembling with fear; but our song was really announcing to all who could hear us—beginning with our own loudly beating hearts—"We will not let our fears overcome us. Neither you with your guns, your dogs, and your terror, nor anything else in the world, will turn us around. Nobody. No way. Never."[15]

Do not be afraid. These words are both an invitation and a promise—an invitation to examine our fears and keep them in perspective, and a promise of God's presence even in terrifying times. Do not just let fear *be*. Feel it, name it, and talk about it when it shows up. But do not allow fear to take over. Do not let it settle in and become your only response to a difficult situation. Relax. Breathe. Invite hope and peace and faith to stand with fear. Even when your heart is pounding with fear, if the cause is worth fighting for, keep marching. The God who chose to comfort Mary desires the same consolation for us in our times of distress, greeting us with the message, do not be afraid.

FINDING FAVOR WITH GOD

"You have found favor with God. And behold, you will conceive in your womb and bear a son, and you shall call his name Jesus" (Lk 1:30–31). Mary speaks four times in Luke's gospel. Her first words are uttered in response to this announcement: "How shall this be, since I have no husband?" (Lk 1:34). Luke's Mary is talking to an angel, an angel sent by God, and she has the audacity to question him! Some news is just too much to unquestioningly accept, even from an angel. Mary is obedient, in the truest sense of the term—*obedire* ("to listen to"). But she is hardly the patriarchal caricature of docility that has often been portrayed by those who like their women acquiescent. Mary of Nazareth's first spoken words in the gospels are words of challenge to the highest religious establishment—an angel sent by God.

Mary represents any woman, any young girl, who faces dire circumstances. She is poor. She is young. She is pregnant. She is confused and alone. Her plight describes tens of thousands of young women in the world today, perhaps even many of us. So does her question: How can this be? It is an expression of disbelief uttered for all the young women and men who cannot believe that the condition in which they find themselves is really happening, much less how they will survive it. It can be an unexpected pregnancy, poverty, homelessness, gnawing hunger, war, imprisonment, divorce, illness, or the grinding weariness that comes from being stuck in a situation from which there seems no relief.

How can this be? It is a perennial question posed by those who stand just this side of denial or perhaps on the precipice of despair: I have worked so hard. How can it be that I have lost my job? My mother has always been so healthy? How can it be that the tests show cancer? My nephew was so young. How can it be that he died? A fifty-year-old women diagnosed with Alzheimer's? No, you have to be kidding! A child with muscular dystrophy? Where is God in this? People dying of starvation? A teenaged woman felled by a police bullet while seeking freedom? 9/11? Katrina? Haiti? How can any of these things happen? Questions of disbelief are posed in the aftermath of any news that sends shock waves through our souls. Anytime something occurs that we are ill prepared to handle, a stunned numbness sets in. Like Mary, we are confused, puzzled, as we struggle to make sense of something that has crashed in upon our lives like an intruder. In Luke's story of the annunciation, Mary's initial reaction is utterly human—it is my reaction and yours. She mounts her argument that such a thing could not possibly be happening. "I have no husband" (Lk 1:34). Shock and denial are normal psychological responses to news that will change our lives in monumental ways. But disaster is not the final word. Mary and God change her tragedy into a love story of epic proportions. But not right away.

We can only interpret Mary of Nazareth as a mystified but readily submissive virgin if we rush past her predicament faster than she did. Rather, we must pause there with her, stay awhile, feel her distress, understand her questioning, and recognize that

the lovely verses we can read in seconds would have taken some
time to grasp, much less accept. Strip away the biblical references to maidens conceiving. Even more important, hear them
on the lips of all the frightened women and men today who encounter unexpected annunciations. Long before an annunciation
becomes a stained-glass window, it is an anguished cry of disbelief. It must be puzzled through before it is memorialized with
oil and canvas or turned into a prayer.

THE ANGEL

Angels painted by the various artists of the annunciation interpret the messenger in varying ways. The angelic presence might
appear friendly or ominous, soft or strong, portly or slender, elderly or utterly childlike. Together they invite us to consider the
many faces and forms that God's message might take in our lives
today. Angels do not conform to a particular pattern.

The word *angel* simply means "messenger." There are some
three hundred references to angelic interventions in the bible. In
Luke's narrative, as well as in other biblical literature, the use of
an angel is a literary device that calls our attention to the caring
presence of God, or to an event in which something significant is
about to happen. Gabriel appears to Daniel, who then proph-
esies the coming of the Messiah and the destruction of the Temple
(Dn 9:21)—an event that had taken place shortly before Luke
was writing his gospel. In another Old Testament vision Gideon
is greeted with a message that matches Gabriel's words to Mary:
"The Lord is with you" (Jgs 6:12). In an annunciation that pre-
cedes and parallels Mary's, Zachariah receives a visit from an angel called Gabriel, announcing that he and his wife Elizabeth,
assumed to be barren, will have a son, whom he is to call John
(Lk 1:11–14). Angels also show up in the Christian literature. At
the end of Jesus' symbolic ordeal in the wilderness, angels come
to minister to him (Mt 4:11). The presence of an angel in scripture always has a similar message: Pay attention. God is here.
Something extraordinary is about to happen.

It is easy to focus more on the messenger than the message, making the angels of scripture literal beings—actual winged creatures sent straight from the heavens. If the annunciation narrative conjures up such ethereal images, we might miss its main point. None of us is likely to receive embodied celestial visitors in our life. But we *will* be visited by the holy bearing messages from God. These messages are the everyday angels, friends whose greeting reminds us that we are graced, sunsets that take our breath away, quiet moments when we are suddenly aware of our profound connectedness to one another and to the other creatures with whom we share our blue water planet. Angels are the "still, strong voice" within us. They are scientists, prophesying global warming, pandemics, or species extinction, warning us to take heed and act. An angel might be the gaunt face of a starving child, the hollow eyes of a lonely elderly man, the blank stare of one weary of yet another war, prompting us to intervene, to be the compassion of the living God for them. Angels make their home in our minds and hearts, interrupting our lives with ideas that call for action in behalf of justice. They live in refugee camps, bombed-out villages, and hospitals where patients and medical personnel alike wait to hear the message: the Lord is with you. Angels sit inside the face of everyone around you.

Gabriel delivers a message meant for each of us. With Mary, we are greeted, learn of God's abiding presence with us, are reminded of our dignity, and are called to bear God's very life in our own times.[16] The messenger will change and the content of the message will vary. But if we listen, as Mary did, if we puzzle over its meaning and ask hard questions, another path for the continuation of God's care in the world will open up.

OVERSHADOW

The Greek word *episkiazo* ("overshadow") is used to describe two events in Jesus' life—his conception and his transfiguration. In each, a mysterious shadowing over by the holy provides confirmation of God's presence. Often described as a hovering cloud, this same protective nearness accompanies the Israelites in their wanderings (Ex 16:10). Wherever the *overshadowing* presence is used in scripture, it always signifies the "Spirit of God drawing near to save and protect."[17]

But the overshadowing of the Holy Spirit is given a new meaning in the annunciation story—or, at least, it is applied differently. Even though overshadowing by the Holy Spirit carries within its imagery no hint of sexual activity, it identifies the way Mary becomes pregnant with her son. Some understand this biblical overshadowing in a literal way, believing that God replaces human paternity for Jesus. Others believe that a human father or an actual male (Y) chromosome would not negate God's gracious action in either Jesus or Mary. The real meaning of the overshadowing at the annunciation is that the Spirit of God, who is always associated with creation, was there, prompting, encouraging, empowering. New life and birth, wherever they happen, are the work of God's hand. There is a mysterious overshadowing of God's spirit that attends the conception of every human being. Holy presence hovers over each of us with divine endorsement from the beginning. To the extent that God authors all life, how could God not be there when it first happens?

EVERYDAY ANNUNCIATIONS

Annunciations are part of our unfolding stories—the sudden appearance of an angel and a virgin called to be the mother of God happens all the time! It takes place when you see a place where a savior is needed and give over part of your life to make a difference. It occurs when you feel insignificant but hear an unexpected summons to help life flourish in one out-of-the-way corner of our planet. Annunciations come about when you wonder how the impossible can flourish, when you ask challenging questions, and when you offer your thoughts in response. Annunciations precede the opening of soup kitchens, clothing collections, and fund drives for the poor. Annunciations send out the word when housing and medical supplies are needed after an earthquake, when schools must be built in remote places, when wars must be ended. Annunciations take place whenever someone or something compels your attention to act in a way that brings about peace, justice, and equality to one household, one neighborhood, one relationship at a time.

An annunciation only needs two things: a message and a recipient. The message need not be lofty, and the recipient need not have high social standing. The message always reads: Will you make love more present in the world? And the recipient always wonders how. She is puzzled at best, or he is terrified at what might be asked. The response from the messenger is always the same: A spirit named Holy will envelop you. You can do this. And—you don't have to be alone. Go and visit Elizabeth, your kinswoman. Community facilitates annunciation.

Chapter 3

Visitation

Meeting One Another on the Inside

> *In those days*
> *Mary arose and went with haste to a Judean town in the hill*
> *country,*
> *where she entered the house of Zechariah*
> *and greeted Elizabeth.*
> *When Elizabeth heard Mary's greeting,*
> *the child leaped in her womb.*
> *And Elizabeth was filled with the Holy Spirit*
> *and exclaimed with a loud cry,*
> *"Blessed are you among women,*
> *and blessed is the fruit of your womb.*
> *And why has this happened to me,*
> *that the mother of my Lord comes to me?*
> *For as soon as I heard the sound of your greeting,*
> *the child in my womb leaped for joy.*
> *And blessed is she who believed that there would be a fulfillment*
> *of what was spoken to her by the Lord." (Lk 1:39–42)*

Two women. Each famous for the child she produces. Each pregnant in a world where giving birth is dangerous to both mother and child and growing from infancy to adulthood is fraught with risk. As if the weight of this is not enough, the babies of both mothers carry in their bones the added burden of a special call.

Each feels compelled, indeed driven, by an inner voice to announce the reign of God. Their personalities are different and their styles divergent, but their commitment is undaunted. Their actions incur the wrath of political and religious authorities. They suffer and are killed for living the life they are born to live. Another mother's heart is broken. How many times has this story unfolded on earth?

BIBLICAL SISTERS

Mary and Elizabeth are two pregnant women in a man's world. It is a world where women are referenced as mothers, wives, and sisters, and not named as persons. In the story of the biblical visitation, however, where the scene involves only two players, both of them women, their names are used several times in a few short lines. Here, briefly, we know these women by name. And we hear them speak without reservation. The house, we are told, is Zechariah's, but he has been struck dumb. He is not a participant in this fast-paced drama that unfolds between Mary and Elizabeth. Theirs are the only voices we hear. "Such quieting of the male voice is highly unusual in scripture."[1] In the absence of patriarchal speech, Mary and Elizabeth talk. But theirs is not ordinary discourse. They proclaim! They speak with excitement and conviction about spiritual matters. As they bring forward memories of women who have gone before them, revelation electrifies their words and the history of God's enduring care for the downtrodden shines through their proclamation. Luke does not give us a superficial visitation composed of idle chatter. His is a rare portrait of two otherwise insignificant women meeting and greeting, touching one another on the inside, and shouting God's goodness. As they boldly utter the beliefs of their hearts, they sing a theology. It is preaching at its soul-stirring best.

What happens to these biblical sisters? We know little about the life or death of Elizabeth after she gives birth to John. The only other time she is mentioned in the Christian writings is at her child's circumcision and naming when she corrects those who want to name him after his father. "No; he is to be called John," she states emphatically, still confident in her own voice (Lk 1:60). "None of your relatives has this name," they argue (Lk 1:61). As the scene continues, they turn predictably to Zechariah. Even though he cannot speak, his patriarchal *authority* has not been silenced. He is given a writing tablet and confirms Elizabeth's words. "His name is John," he writes decisively (Lk 1:63). In a swift display of male supremacy, the matter is settled. Even though Zechariah cannot talk, he has the last word. After he regains his ability to speak, we do not hear again from Elizabeth. By the time Luke turns his attention to her now-grown son, John the Baptist is introduced as "John son of Zechariah" (Lk 3:2). Elizabeth, poet and prophet, spirit-filled preacher well versed in the writings of her people, has disappeared altogether from her son's lineage.

Have you ever felt left out, even though you had contributed something vital to a project or a conversation? Have your talents ever been ignored?

> In college, a play I wrote was selected for performance by the drama club. In the program, they omitted my name as the author, but identified all the actors in bold letters. I felt bad about it, sort of passed over. My grandmother told me just to forget it because women should be happy to be in the background.[2]

Elizabeth, the mother of John the Baptist who also faded into the background, would have understood. Even though she lived two thousand years earlier, some attitudes have remained the same.

Mary of Nazareth, the young woman who figures so prominently in the nativity narratives, merits only occasional mention later in the life of the child she brought forth. Often, her presence is recounted without using her name. In the gospel of John, Mary is *never* mentioned by name, even though two lengthy conversations between Jesus and his mother are recorded. Like so many mothers who offer an eager womb and a lifetime of sacrifice to their children, Mary and Elizabeth were not expecting personal greatness. They nursed their baby boys, taught them to walk and talk, and hummed lullabies to them in the night, all the while hoping that their sons would be met with goodness instead of calamity as they made their way in the world. They pondered the sword so often aimed at the hearts of mothers— hoping it might pass them by. It didn't.

BIBLICAL BACKGROUND

The story of the visitation is embedded in the nativity narratives to serve Luke's theological purpose. Some scholars have understood it as an epilogue to the annunciation, in which Mary, as first and model disciple, fulfills "with haste" the first duty of discipleship by visiting Elizabeth, thus sharing the gospel with others.[3] Like the account of the annunciation, the visitation is rich in Hebrew imagery, created by Luke to bring John the Baptist and Jesus together before either of them is even born. From the beginning, within his mother's womb, John the Baptist recognizes Jesus and alerts others to his presence.[4] Elizabeth identifies Mary as the mother of the Messiah, whose coming will be good news for the lowly and the poor. Once again, the most unlikely of characters are chosen to figure prominently in God's plan. It starts with women—spirit-filled pregnant prophets.[5]

The theological import of Luke's message is lost if the story of the visitation is understood literally. Such a reading strips the story of its deepest meaning and erases its powerful Hebrew symbolism, leaving us with only an outline of improbable, uninspired events. The Judean hill country, the place Elizabeth and Zechariah lived, was about a four-day journey south of Nazareth, where Mary lived. Walking between the two places was the mode of transportation for the peasant population. When people did make this arduous journey, they joined with other travelers, both for safety and companionship. It is highly doubtful that a teenage girl, newly pregnant, would suddenly undertake a four-day journey alone into the Judean hill country. As the Catholic biblical scholar Robert J. Karris attests, it "strains credulity to imagine a fourteen-year-old Jewish virgin making a four-day journey by herself."[6] Brown also notes that the story of the visitation is not about a charitable visit, whereby a young girl goes to help her pregnant kinswoman. Even if Mary had undertaken a literal visit to Elizabeth, it is unlikely that she would depart for home three months later, just as Elizabeth, by now nine months pregnant, would most need the attendance of other women. In the world of pregnant women, one does not leave the other just as a birth is imminent.

So if the teenaged, pregnant Mary did not undertake a *literal* visit to Elizabeth, how do we understand the meaning of the visitation? First, it can be helpful if we read this beautiful and poetic story with a bible in one hand and a good biblical commentary in the other.[7] Only then, with an understanding of its theological setting, can we more deeply appreciate the powerful narrative, this imaginative retelling about two women who are pregnant and who, in meeting and greeting one another, come to a fuller understanding of how God is present in their story.[8]

SHE WENT WITH HASTE

The word in Greek is *spoude* ("haste"). It is the same word Luke uses to describe the journey of the shepherds as they went *with haste* to find Mary and Joseph with their newborn babe, lying in a manger (Lk 2:16). Biblical haste *(spoude)* involves eagerness, an expectation that something important awaits at the end of the journey. The word, which can also be translated "earnestness" or "earnest care," puts us on notice that this is no casual undertaking. However Mary might have heard of Elizabeth's pregnancy, her thoughts rushed toward her. Her caring was with her. We can think of Mary's travel to her kinswoman as a true journey of the heart.

It should be the same for us whenever we meet one another. We ought to enter every significant human encounter with care, with intention, with thoughtfulness. The greetings we exchange, the words we share have power—power to comfort, power to heal, power to cause insides to quiver. There is no room for carelessness in our interactions with others. Approaching one another with mediocrity does not stir a lagging spirit or lift us up to joy. The *haste* of Mary's journey to Elizabeth depicts *energy*— sparks of power that charged their encounter with recognition of the goodness that each carried in her body. The same holy energy is carried within each of us. When we journey *with haste*, that is, with earnest care, toward one another, each of our meetings effects visitation once again.

SHE ENTERED THE HOUSE

When we truly connect, we enter the interior space of one another. Here, the space that Mary enters is described as a house (*oikos*, in Greek). We usually think of a *house* as a physical place, but it can also refer to that deep interior center of each person, often identified as the *self* or the *soul*. In Greek, the word *oikos* can also be translated "sanctuary." Indeed, each of us, as *imago Dei*, is a sanctuary, an abode of the holy. We even refer to human beings as "dwelling places" of the divine. In moments of genuine intimacy, my truest, deepest self *enters into* the truest, deepest self of another—we journey "inside of" one another's houses. At such times we have entered a place not bound by walls or separated by doors. Here, in this most personal and sacred of interior spaces, we have access to the private feelings, thoughts, and experiences of the other. These types of interior meeting, such soul-to-soul encounters, represent the most profound of all levels of human union. We are all little chapels walking around providing a traveling home for the God who is always on a journey, awaiting the next visitation.

We are told that Mary entered an *oikos* that belonged to Zechariah—Zechariah the currently silent patriarchal husband and property owner. But it was not Zechariah whom Mary met, it was Elizabeth, her formerly barren kinswoman. Elizabeth had been hiding:

> *After these days his wife Elizabeth conceived,*
> *and for five months she hid herself, saying,*

"Thus the Lord has done to me in the days when he looked on me,
to take away my reproach among men." (Lk 1:24–25)

A comparison with Elizabeth's biblical counterpart, Hannah (1 Sm
1:1–18) reveals the heartbreaking plight of barren women in Israel. God had promised that Abram's descendants would outnumber the stars (Gn 15:5–6). Women participate in this divine plan by having children, particularly sons. But how does
the barren woman claim a vital role in fulfilling God's promise?
Since it was believed that God was in charge of opening and
closing women's wombs, a "closed womb" was a sign of God's
rebuke, or possibly punishment. A barren woman was scorned
or even taunted by women who had born children, as was
Hannah (1 Sm 1:6). A source of embarrassment both to herself
and her husband, the barren woman carried a triple sadness:
public shame, abandonment by God, and the lonely grief of an
empty cradle. Any one of them would have been reason enough
to hide.

When Mary enters the house that day, she meets a woman
familiar with hiding. Since seclusion during pregnancy was not a
custom in Israel, Elizabeth's hiding is interpreted in some other
way. Theologically, it is likely a Lucan literary device intended to
more closely connect the birth of John the Baptist with that of
Jesus.[9] But within the drama of the narrative, and the wisdom of
women's ways of knowing, many explanations are possible. Accustomed as she was to the stigma of sterility, after years of waiting, yearning, praying, Elizabeth might have needed time to savor her conception, to reflect on its meaning, even to be sure of
it before venturing out to face the questions and comments of
others. Pregnant with a hope so new, a woman in Elizabeth's time
might have felt more comfortable staying out of the public eye
until her pregnancy was visible to all. By the end of five months,
she could go out into the streets and end her public disgrace.[10]
By then, her swelling belly would make the announcement for
her: Her reproach would be ended! As with Sarah and Hannah
before her, God has looked with compassion on a woman's plight
and once again done the impossible.

But we can find in Elizabeth's hiding yet another meaning. Women of her time, barren or not, were constrained to certain roles. They could work in the fields and go about the village, but they could not participate in the highest level of religious leadership. Their duties were limited to the *oikos* of the house, and did not involve the *oikos* of the synagogue or Temple. The house of God was inhabited by men. Elizabeth, like her husband Zechariah, came from the priestly family of Aaron. Yet, as a woman, she would never have the opportunity her husband had—to be selected to burn incense at the altar in the Temple. Only priests, all of them male, could enter into such a holy place. Even a speechless man like Zechariah, who could not complete the ritual of evening sacrifice by blessing the people, was more acceptable as a religious leader than a woman. So Elizabeth's hiding was also a symbolic seclusion, shared by all women, as a result of being female. That deeply spiritual part of Elizabeth that could intuit the presence of the holy and burst forth in blessing had remained hidden. Until now. When she opened the door to her visitor, she also opened it to herself.

Do you know what it feels like—to have a gift and not be able to use it because circumstances or institution forbid its expression? To hold words of blessing within your heart, sermons ripe for hearing, that must remain concealed? Elizabeth stands for all women and men who are hidden behind burkas and veils, protocols and exclusions, poverty and disability. She is every young person whose situation prevents education, every competent woman who stands forever in the shadow of a less competent male CEO, every married man who hears a call to priesthood, and every woman who hears the same call, regardless of her life state. Elizabeth represents the part of you that remains unseen because of shyness or fear, the part that stays undeveloped because some barrier prevents its flourishing. Her story stands as witness to God's desire for everyone who is obscure, held back and held down, confined and oppressed: *Go to the door. I am sending a visitor whose greeting will make your heart leap for joy.* That visitor is you. It is me. It is each of us who hears the call to go out of our way, to make a dangerous journey to invite our brothers and sisters into the light.

GREETING, HEARING, LEAPING

Mary enters the house and greets Elizabeth. Though custom would suggest an emotional reunion between two kinswomen who had likely not seen one another in some time, Luke is not interested in displaying it. He needs to get Mary and Elizabeth together for his larger theological purpose. The Greek word *aspasmos* means "greeting." In Luke's theology of the visitation, the excitement hinges on this word. Mary, the visitor, the pregnant teenage traveler, extends the *greeting* and sets the stage for a prenatal theophany. Elizabeth hears her greeting. John, the babe in Elizabeth's womb, in his sixth month of gestation, recognizes the presence of the holy one within Mary's womb and "leaps" an early birth announcement. As they listen to the story of the visitation, the hearers of Luke's gospel can be sure that John, who will be known as the Baptist, has identified Jesus. Luke's purpose is fulfilled.

But must we take our leave as quickly as Mary did, so the curtain can open on the next act of Luke's sacred drama? Or might we linger a while in Zechariah's house in search of a metaphor for our lives? Can we meet these women on another level, one that stands alongside Luke's theology but also extends it? How are Mary and Elizabeth like us? How do we identify with them so that their story becomes our story?[11] As Luke portrays the relationship between Mary and Elizabeth, an exquisite attunement shines between them. Mary greets; Elizabeth hears. Mary's greeting penetrates Elizabeth to the depth of her pregnant womb. She hears and internalizes the greeting so completely that something powerful stirs within her. It touches the core of her being—that sanctuary where the deepest self resides. She could not miss it. She knows its name and calls it holy.

As instantly as Elizabeth hears, the babe in her womb leaps—Elizabeth's hearing is synonymous with the response of her child. Elizabeth's hearing is John's hearing. This kind of instantaneous interior responsiveness is not unusual among pregnant women and their babies. We have long known that the earliest fetal response to sound is at twenty-six weeks. Babies can also intuit and react to the emotional responses of their mothers, as well as to the responses of others around them. The rapid interplay between Mary's greeting, Elizabeth's hearing, and John's response is a reminder of the wondrous and mysterious communication between mother and child in the womb.

Fetal development, of course, is not Luke's concern as he crafts his visitation scene. He does not need gestational movement to convince his first-century hearers that the yet unborn John was already identifying the one whose sandal he would not be fit to untie (Lk 3:16). Elizabeth's son is ushering in a new way of understanding God's reign. And it is happening with the most unlikely and helpless of characters: pregnant women and their unborn children. The youngest and most dependent among us witness the holy.

WHEN ELIZABETH HEARD

It is hearing so acute that both Elizabeth and John have a visceral response to Mary's greeting. Their depth of perception is foundational to recognizing and proclaiming Mary's son. But this kind of hearing belongs not only to the characters in Luke's visitation. It also represents human interaction at its healthiest, at its holiest, in each of us. The ability to hear—to attend so closely that a message from another affects our hearts, sinks inside and changes how we live—will be a primary characteristic of discipleship when Jesus begins his public ministry.

For Jesus, true hearing is connected to living in accord with the word of God. When he is preaching, a woman from the crowd says to him: "Blessed is the womb that bore you, and the breasts that you sucked!" But he said, "Blessed rather are those who hear the word of God and obey it!" (Lk 11:27–28).

It is not wombs and breasts, isolated from persons, that make women blessed—no matter how great the children they have nurtured. The cause for blessedness does not reside in body parts. The woman in the crowd calls out a proclamation of praise for a mother typical in her day. But Jesus has a propensity for confronting commonly accepted practices that diminish the dignity of persons. Blessedness, he challenges, is not the automatic result of bearing and nursing children, but rather, of *hearing and obeying* God's word. Other authors have pointed out that Mary is being identified in this story as woman who has, in fact, heard and kept the word of God.[12] This is what makes her blessed. It is the source of her discipleship.

Had Elizabeth heard this message earlier, perhaps her sadness at being barren would not have carried the added sting of disgrace. She, a woman, a barren woman, can be holy, indeed blessed, even if she does not contribute to the descendants that outnumber the stars—another metaphor not to be taken literally! Jesus' retort to the woman in the crowd lifts all women out of a narrow, patriarchal role and offers them the possibility of discipleship based not on bearing children but on hearing and keeping God's word. This was something Elizabeth could do, with or without conception! It is something each of us can do.

FILLED WITH THE HOLY SPIRIT

A favorite expression of Luke's, being filled with the Holy Spirit, signifies God's empowering presence. It enables action that flows from the divine. The use of the phrase is often paired with momentous events when God's holy energy is particularly needed. It is used of Jesus at critical junctures of his ministry. When he is baptized by John in the Jordan, the "Holy Spirit descended upon him" (Lk 3:22), leaving him "full of the Holy Spirit" (Lk 4:1). It is a presence that will not abandon him. When Jesus comes out of the wilderness experience, "in the power of the Spirit" (Lk 4:14), he has become so certain of the sustaining presence of this Spirit named Holy that he will continue to act in its name (Lk 4:18–19).

By the time Luke creates the nativity narratives, Jesus has preached and healed, died and risen. Pentecost has taken place. The Holy Spirit has been there for all of it. It makes good theological sense that Luke will "fill with the Holy Spirit" the main characters of the visitation. It will show continuity between the present and the future and further convince his hearers that the ever-hovering spirit of God has been breathing on their history from the beginning.

WOMEN GREETING AND BLESSING

Elizabeth is the first character in the visitation scene that Luke pronounces "filled with the Holy Spirit" (Lk 1:42). Like many other spirit-filled people, hers is a fullness that cannot not be suppressed. For Elizabeth, as she connects profoundly with Mary's greeting, feeling it dance through her body, there is nothing to do but shout! Suddenly, all the patriarchal constraints fall away from this pregnant woman of the spirit, and she bursts forth in blessing.

Though there is mention of other women in Israel's history who have prophetic roles, or who offer and receive blessings, they are typically women acting in roles usually reserved for men. Huldah, a prophet known for her mercy, is consulted for an opinion when the king desires a compassionate response, even though there are male prophets in the area (2 Kgs 22:14–19). Deborah is the leader of an army who pronounces Jael blessed after she kills Israel's enemy by driving a tent peg through his skull with such force that it enters the ground beneath his head (Jgs 5:24–27). Judith wins a blessing from Uzziah for saving Israel by decapitating Holophernes (Jdt 13:23–24). Although the words of the blessings in these scenes echo those of Elizabeth for Mary, the settings are entirely different. While praise of female leaders in Israel's history is associated with action that is understood to represent God's saving power for the people, much of it takes place in the context of violence, sexual wiles, and trickery. Jael and Judith would probably not be the first biblical women who would come to mind as we think of apt contemporary models of holiness for our daughters!

By contrast, Elizabeth's double blessing in the visitation scene has none of the typical bloody carnage, sexual guile, or military victory associated with others of Israel's female leaders and prophets. Elizabeth blesses Mary not for taking life but for giving it. A new age of peace is being ushered in as Elizabeth interprets Mary's significance for God's people. Although Luke never gives Elizabeth the title of prophet, "she functions like one."[13] Authentic prophets are those who speak in God's name. They serve as the voice of the holy for the people. When they speak, the message is not theirs but God's. When Elizabeth bursts into words of poetic blessing, she is presented as one in touch with the mind of God. It is God's blessing, the fullness of the Holy Spirit, at work through her voice. A woman's words. God's proclamation.

BLESSED AMONG WOMEN

"The Queen of Heaven Is Coming to Town!" These striking words announced a Marian Conference in a full-page advertisement in a Seattle newspaper in the 1990s. The title Queen of Heaven, assigned to Mary of Nazareth in modern times, originally belonged to the pagan goddess in one of her many forms. The accompanying newspaper photo, ostensibly of Mary, bore striking resemblance to ancient images of Astarte, also known as Divine Mother. Jeremiah references the cult of the goddess as he bemoans the inability of the people to abandon their practice of worshiping them:

> *The children gather wood, the fathers kindle fire,*
> *and the women knead dough, to make cakes for the queen of heaven,*
> *and they pour out drink offerings to other gods,*
> *to provoke me to anger. (Jer 7:18)*

Over the years, Mary has been adorned with the crown and given the titles formerly belonging to the pagan goddess—something Jeremiah would likely bemoan as much today as then. Mary has also been set apart, presented as "most blessed" among all women.[14] Some have suggested that elevating Mary to heavenly status fulfills a subconscious need for female symbolism for the deity, especially for Roman Catholics, where God, priests, and leaders are all male. Whatever the reason, Mary of Nazareth has gradually been stripped of much that makes her a real flesh-and-blood woman as esoteric dogmas about her conception, perpetual virginity, and assumption have been assigned to her. This has put her on a star-studded pedestal, removing her from her peasant roots and from the ordinary life she lived in Nazareth before and after the birth of her son. The real Mary of Nazareth, the mother of Jesus, the wife of Joseph, is only a minor player in the gospels; her death is not even recorded. She is never spoken of in scripture with any of the lofty titles accorded the goddesses of the Greco-Roman world until a cult around her memory began to develop in the early church.[15] While Elizabeth addresses Mary as "the mother of my Lord" (Lk 1:43), the appellation is not about conveying a title to Mary, but about Luke's post-resurrection introduction of Jesus to the Gentile Christians. The references in the book of Revelation about a woman clothed with the sun (Rv 12:1–2) were not originally attributed to Mary.

This is certainly not to suggest that Mary is not blessed. But she is blessed *among women*, not above women. She stands in the midst of all women (and men) who listen to God in their lives and respond with courage to what is asked of them. She is blessed because of God's favor, the same favor offered to each of us. Anything that removes Mary from her place *among women* ensures that she will be venerated but not emulated as a mother, friend, sister, and lover.

How do you think of Mary? Do you admire her courage in asking hard questions of authority figures? For her ability to think through terrifying dilemmas and make life-giving choices? Do you remember her youthful capacity to claim her power and dignity as the graced daughter of a holy God? Do you honor her as a mother, for being there for her child, often in the background, as he confronts his life choices? We do not know what happened to Joseph, Mary's husband. But if Mary did become a widow, as some scholars suspect, do you marvel at her ability to remember who she is in a world where women receive their identity from their fathers and husbands? Do you stand in awe of her for staying at the cross to the bitter end, even after the less brave had left? These things identify Mary as blessed and enable her to be a true model for women and men in difficult circumstances everywhere.

EVERYDAY VISITATION

Who of us, upon hearing that a beloved relative or friend is pregnant after years of trying to have a child, would not make contact as quickly as possible? What fantastic news! A baby! After all these years! The impulse to connect would be strong and deep. We would want to enter into the joy and be immersed in the excitement as quickly as possible—not tomorrow, or next week, but *now*! That is what the promise of new life evokes in us. Today, we would probably pull out our phone and hit the speed-dial number. We would intuitively feel what Mary felt, and we would want to connect—*with haste*.

It has always been that way with women. There is something about the news of a pregnancy that awakens wonder in each of us, even if we have never borne a child. It is news that is not easily silenced. Whether a long-awaited pregnancy or an unintended one, the need to talk about it can be as urgent as the growing belly. And who but another expectant mother, or someone who has borne a child, could better understand the mix of emotions at such an event? For both the older woman and the younger one, excitement mingles with apprehension. The urgency to talk, to let fears spill out, and to raise questions is as strong as the bond that inspires the tedious travel that brings them to this place in their lives.

Theirs is a necessary visit. A woman's journey through a pregnancy was, and still is, dangerous. Perhaps the story of the visitation has become a Christian feast day because it evokes some deep level of recognition in each of us. We understand the feelings that lie beneath the story line. Women and men alike can truly enter into this story and make it their own.

It is not only a pregnancy that invites us into visitation. There is a strong urge in the human heart to seek direct contact at important times of life and death, celebration and loss. We gravitate toward those we trust whenever emotional intensity enters our lives. It is perhaps not surprising that the great feasts in all world religions are associated with travel, with going to see loved ones. The visitation is a symbol of that profound urge to journey to others, especially at those times when something of consequence is being memorialized. In the very act of meeting, energies are joined and bonds are formed that empower our future journeys.

THE VISITATION AS LITURGY

The flow of events is simple but potent: Mary goes with haste. She enters the house. She greets Elizabeth. Elizabeth hears Mary. The child in Elizabeth's womb "leaps." Elizabeth is filled with a sense of the holy. She proclaims a blessing upon Mary. Mary responds.

Entering. Greeting. Hearing. Feeling. Blessing. Responding. The simple visit of these two women offers us a vivid example of the structure of healthy/holy human encounter. It gives us a glimpse of what can unfold when we meet one another on the inside. Though words are few, and details of this biblical visitation are spare, when Mary takes her leave, both women are more aware of who they are, before one another and before God. They have claimed their voices and been heard. They are blessed. That is what true meeting ought to effect in us each time we come together.

Mary and Elizabeth align themselves with other women in Hebrew history as they sing their songs to each other. Their voices recall those of Miriam, who led all the women in singing and dancing as the people crossed the Red Sea (Ex 15:20–21). They particularly echo the exultant prayer of Hannah after the formerly barren woman is blessed with a son, Samuel, and offers him to God: "My heart exults in the Lord; my strength is exalted in my God" (1 Sm 2:1). In remembering their sisters from the past they remind themselves and us that God continues from age to age to lift up the lowly, to extend favor to the downtrodden. As they recount God's deeds in behalf of those most oppressed they bring God's compassion forward in time. The memories help them pass on God's favor to each other and remind us that we can do the same today.

The tender and loving story of the visit between two women, swelling with God's creative life, has all the elements of good liturgy. The scene opens with a greeting and a response. The word is proclaimed: "Blessed is the fruit of your womb!" Its meaning brings joy. Nourished by their shared encounter at the table that is their lives, the women are filled, both in womb and being. There is one more closing blessing. They will depart from this place strengthened for the journey, and the labor, that lie ahead.

The energy in the story evokes imagery of the best liturgy. Coming together from different places, different lives, meeting, singing, remembering the stories that feed us—when liturgy has these elements, it is like a pregnant womb, a storehouse of life for the journey. Mary and Elizabeth are model celebrants of this early celebration of eucharistic life. As they stand at the altar of their lives, they help us remember that our lives are also holy tables, places where our words can evoke hope, where our bodies nourish life, where we bless one another's continuation on the road ahead.

Chapter 4

Nativity

Giving Birth in Unexpected Places

Matthew: The Nativity Story
When Joseph awoke from sleep, he did as the angel of the Lord
commanded him;
he took her as his wife,
but had no marital relations with her until she had borne a son,
and he named him Jesus.
In the time of King Herod, after Jesus was born in Bethlehem of
Judea,
wise men from the East came to Jerusalem, asking,
"Where is the child who has been born king of the Jews?
For we observed his star at its rising,
and have come to pay him homage." . . .
On entering the house,
they saw the child with Mary his mother;
and they knelt down and paid him homage.
(Mt 1:24—2:2; 2:11)

Luke: The Nativity Story
While they were there,
the time came for her to deliver her child.
And she gave birth to her firstborn son
and wrapped him in bands of cloth,

53

and laid him a manger,
because there was no place for them in the inn.
In that region there were shepherds living in the fields,
keeping watch over their flock by night.
Then an angel of the Lord stood before them,
and the glory of the Lord shone around them,
and they were terrified.

(Lk 2:6–9)

NEEDING CHRISTMAS

We always unpacked the old hand-carved nativity set carefully
and put it on a table next to the Christmas tree. Over the years
the stable became worn, the figures chipped. Sheep were missing
legs, and the cow had only one horn. Or was it an ox? One poor
angel was wingless, and a shepherd had to stand in for Joseph,
who had become lost somewhere in the attic. By the time I was in
high school, our three original wise men had been reduced by
two, and the neck of the baby Jesus was ringed in hardened glue
where his head had been reattached numerous times. But our
wounded little nativity set never lost its capacity to fill us with a
sense of expectation. Perhaps there was something about its missing and damaged parts that signaled a need for Christmas once
again.

Angels and wise men. Shepherds and stars. It never occurred
to us as children that we were mixing metaphors as we mixed the
images in the two different nativity accounts in the gospels. Mangers, shepherds, and crowded inns belong only to Luke, who
doesn't mention Matthew's wise men or their traveling star—
much less tell us that there are three wise men. But this was Christmas, the most enchanting of Christian feasts, brought forward in
time through tangible, visual symbols that were important less
for their biblical accuracy than for their power to rekindle our
wonder and stir our hearts. Along with strains of "Silent Night"
and "Adeste Fideles" playing softly in the background, our family nativity set reminded us, every winter of our lives, of the birth
that provided the foundation of our faith.

A NATIVITY STORY TOLD FROM THE PAST

When Matthew and Luke crafted their exquisite nativity stories, they were each "equally interested in connecting Jesus' birth with the ancient traditions of his people's sacred writings."[1] Drawing from biblical accounts of other saving events like that of Moses (Ex 2:5–6), previous angelic birth announcements (the unnamed wife of Manoah (Jgs 13:2–7), and earlier miraculous interventions (1 Sm 1:19–20), Matthew and Luke elicit faith in Jesus by instructing their readers that God is acting in Jesus in the same way God has acted in the past. Just as we repeated our annual nativity ritual, the evangelists knew that unpacking old stories would reinforce their message about how God acts.

The two different birth stories of Jesus in the gospels were not designed to be joined together, but to evoke recognition in the reader. In both Israelite and Hellenistic worlds people were accustomed to "miraculous events accompanying the birth-accounts of extraordinary people."[2] Matthew, writing predominantly for Jewish Christian readers, can readily draw from stories in the Hebrew writings and Jewish traditions without having to explain them. Once upon a time, according to Matthew, a baby boy was born. He was a special child, sent by God to save his people. But his life was threatened by a plot to massacre all the baby boys born in the land. The child's life was spared, and he grew up in the sight of God. This, of course, is the bare bones story of Moses' birth, which was planted in the hearts and memories of the Israelite people (Ex 1—2). Counting on these sacred memories, Matthew fashions an account of Jesus' birth using elements of the story of Moses in order to show that Jesus is in continuity with other holy people sent by God to save them. Jesus is the new Moses.

Luke needs a different story. Writing primarily for Gentile Christians who are less familiar with Israel's sacred stories, Luke emphasizes Jesus' universal humanity in the midst of his divine origins. Once upon a time, according to Luke, a real human person named Mary gave birth to a baby boy while she and her betrothed, Joseph, were away from home, having been forced to go to Bethlehem because of a decree from the emperor. Mary laid the baby in a manger because the inn was full. Because he was the Son of God, angels appeared to announce his birth to shepherds in the nearby fields. Luke's nativity account emphasizes the humble origins of this human/divine child. He is born on a journey, without any trappings of royalty. A heavenly host singing out his welcome ensures that Luke's hearers will know who he is, but shepherds, dirty from the fields, will also remind them that this is a savior who will receive everyone.

Stepping back from the details of the nativity accounts, it is easy to see how they function as imaginative retellings, or sacred myths, to help early Christians better understand who Jesus is and what significance his story holds for their lives. Matthew's audience takes comfort in hearing the connection between Jesus and their ancestors. Their faith can be strengthened knowing that theirs is a God who keeps promises, who will never leave them. That is far more important to them than verifying the details of Jesus' first visitors. Luke's readers are consoled to know that the God of the Israelites is also their God, that in Jesus, God has expanded the guest list to the banquet. This is indeed good news!

Biblical scholars and theologians have examined the details of both nativity stories word by word, line by line, adding much clarity regarding their sources and depth of understanding about their meaning.[3] It is not my purpose to summarize that scholarly research, but rather to assume it and draw upon it where needed in order to explore the symbolism of the stories from the perspective of psychology.

ONCE UPON A BIRTH

How are these birth stories our stories? Perhaps one of the first messages we can take from the accounts of Jesus' nativity is that each of us has a nativity as well—a birth story that holds within it all the promise and hope that attended that Christmas some two thousand years ago. Whatever excitement or sorrow your birth story holds, whatever ordinariness surrounds it, it is worth know-ing and celebrating. What kind of journey of faith were your parents walking when they were waiting for you? How crowded was the inn when you arrived? Who were your first visitors? What expectations were placed on you—expectations that you would only discover much later?

When we were children growing up in the Pacific Northwest, one of the gifts our parents gave us was a special narration of our birth story—every year—on our birthday. After the candles were blown out and a slice of homemade birthday cake had been served to everyone, our mother would begin: "Dad, do you remember when Janee was born? The sun was just coming up when we left for the hospital." Sometimes our father would start: "Mother, I was just remembering the morning Jason was born. I fixed Campbell's turkey noodle soup when I got home from the hospi-tal. It was Thanksgiving Day, so it seemed we should have some-thing with turkey in it!" On Robert's birthday they recounted how the doctor kept him in the hospital because he had a slight rash on his face. After being home only one night, Mom and Dad went to get him "first thing" the next morning. "I just couldn't sleep, thinking about Robert being there without us," Mom al-ways said. And Dad would nod in agreement.

Each of us heard our personal nativity story annually, at least into high school, and occasionally in our adult life. Paul repeat-edly cheered whenever Mom described how she was awake for her entire labor and delivery with him—as if it was some feat for which he was personally responsible. And he cheered again on my birthday upon hearing that her labor with me had been more prolonged. Over the years the narratives were embellished as they were told and retold, and as each of us chimed in with our par-ticular memories of a sibling's birth. None of us would forget the impromptu parade we held down our quiet street, banging on pots and pans to alert the neighbors on the June afternoon when Dad called to tell us we had a new baby sister!

But some things always remained the same. When the storytelling was over, and the birth event had been retold to the satisfaction of our parents, we usually lingered around the table

for a few moments. I remember it as a time of quiet awe—a re-
flective moment, a sacred time. It was as if an angel of the Lord
had visited us, once again bringing news of great joy and leaving
the glory of the Lord shining all around us. It must be what angels do whenever a child is born. Or when a birth is remembered.

GIVING BIRTH AGAIN

Matthew and Luke agree about one detail of the first Christmas—that a young girl named Mary gave birth to a child who
would heal the world. He carried in his being the hopes of all
nations. When Mary said, "Let it be done to me according to
your word" (Lk 1:38), something new was started that did not
end in a manger in Bethlehem or on a cross at Golgotha. A child
was born, to be sure, but like the great genesis that flung forth
stars at the dawn of creation, the fruit of Mary's womb initiated
something that still groans for completion (Rom 8:22). With her
spirited *fiat*, she agreed to deliver a *vision* as much as an infant.

Let my life unfold according to your word. Let your way find
a growing space in me. They are Mary's words and ours. Her son
inherits the promise she made in his DNA—a promise born more
of trust than of clarity. She had no way of anticipating how this
Word of God would make itself known or what it would ask either of her or her child. The angel departed from her as soon as
she uttered the syllables that set the vision in motion. From then
on, there were no more angelic encouragements for Mary—just
an unrecorded pregnancy for a young peasant girl who clung with
all her might to her fresh memory of God's promise from the
ages, just as many of us do in our time. Her commitment is the
beginning of a new articulation of God's dream for humanity.
The child that is born is unusual in more ways than one. An ancient passion stirs within him that will not be silenced. It is a
passion for justice, a vision of a table big enough for everyone,
especially those who most need a banquet. His is a vision that cannot be delivered in a single nativity. It is carried forward in births
not yet completed. This is where his story and ours converge.

Each of us has been overshadowed by the spirit of God and given the task of carrying the vision of the way of God toward fullness. It is a vision of inclusivity and abundance, a dream of oneness where all of God's sons and daughters work together to bring about a universe of justice. The biblical authors spell out the details of this dream using striking images and gripping metaphors throughout the Hebrew and Christian writings: inclusion, justice, peace.

Inclusion

As the dream of God is realized, the most unlikely of creatures share food and pasture. Isaiah gives perhaps the most vivid description of life lived in accord with this vision:

> *The wolf shall live with the lamb,*
> *the leopard shall lie down with the kid,*
> *the calf and the lion and the fatling together,*
> *and a little child shall lead them.*
> *The cow and the bear shall graze,*
> *their young shall lie down together;*
> *and the lion shall eat straw like the ox. (Is 11:6–7)*

In a striking pairing of opposites, wolves and lambs live with one another as companions. Leopards and young goats rest peacefully together, while the cow and bear graze side by side in the same pasture, teaching their young that everyone belongs and no one is harmed. The most dramatic of Isaiah's descriptions of a "new creation," illustrated again in an apocalyptic-style vision in trito-Isaiah (Is 65:17–25), is the taming of the ferocious lion. In Hebrew writings the lion is frequently mentioned as a bold, devouring beast, "the mightiest among wild animals" (Prv 30:30). A symbol of all that is dangerous and predatory, the mighty lion no longer tears flesh, but eats the straw of the ox when the future vision comes into fullness—making true communion a reality.

The imagery is evocative, and the symbolism is ripe for diverse interpretation. Grazing lambs and kids are the prey of flesh-eating wolves and leopards; fatlings are ready for slaughter. In Isaiah's vision of a new creation, adversaries turn into allies, the vulnerable are victims no longer, and territorialism is transformed into a welcome space for all. That which is dangerous becomes safe, while the impossible comes to pass. Isaiah's far-reaching vision is an invitation to break down the barriers of separation and to envision wildly new ways of relating in the human community, indeed, the cosmos. The vision invites each of us to examine places both in our personal lives and in our world where obstacles of prejudice and exclusion lock others out of relationship and community.

Justice

Central to the realization of God's hope for humanity is justice. But justice, in the anticipated flourishing of God's way, is not about retribution or punishment for wrongdoing. Rather, it involves bringing about *right relationship* throughout the human community. The concept of biblical justice undergoes profound transformative development in the Hebrew and Christian scriptures.[4] It is the prophet Micah who highlights the centrality of biblical justice in God's vision most simply. He sees that the rich are taking advantage of the poor, that the powerful are oppressing the disadvantaged, that hostility is being directed against "those who pass by trustingly with no thought of war" (Mi 2:8), and that the religious leaders are mistreating and controlling the people in God's name. When the offenders pledge to make up for their misdeeds by bowing down in prayer, giving rivers of oil and more burnt offerings to God, and even sacrificing their firstborn, Micah ignores their manipulative appeal and solemnly reminds them that they have been told again and again what God requires of them:

> *What is good has been explained to you;*
> *this is what Yahweh asks of you:*
> *only this, to act justly,*
> *to love tenderly*
> *and to walk humbly with your God. (Mi 6:8, JB)*

This unadorned mandate appears in multiple ways throughout the bible. As straightforward as the concept is, it has proven
easier to quote than to put into practice. Justice, love, and humility—the Ten Commandments abbreviated, the Great Commandment fleshed out. These are not rules to keep or laws to enforce;
they are directives for the heart, impulses toward a way of life
that summarize the significance of incarnation. When you and I
act with justice, love with tenderness, and walk with humility, the
holy is given new birth. God's way in the universe has another
chance.

Peace

Finally, the vision awaiting new birth is one of peace. In God's
dream for humanity, spears and swords no longer pierce the hearts
of mothers. They are beat into plowshares and pruning hooks to
till the earth and make food for the banquet (Is 2:4). Weapons
and wars are unfamiliar in God's reign of peace because "nation
shall not lift up sword against nation, neither shall they learn of
war anymore" (Is 2:4). These words from the prophet Isaiah are
forceful. Preparing for war and manufacturing weapons are not
part of God's vision. As long as these tools of battle are present,
anywhere in the world, all disciples carry within them a commission to work to replace the violence of war with the peace of
God's true reign.

The vision that Isaiah offers is a meditation on an idealized
future extending throughout the cosmos—a future dependent
upon knowledge of God's way, which leads to justice, which in
turn is the threshold of peace. That ideal is to be a light in the
darkness, beckoning us toward the reality it so powerfully symbolizes in image and poetry.

Christmas is often called the season of peace—even among
those who do not identify as Christian. It is a time when truces
are called, old hostilities are set aside and the night sky is scanned
for some sign of a star coming to rest over our homes. There
seems to be a collective need the world over to believe in the
possibility of wolves and lambs lying together, at least for a day.

Carols of the season sing of peace-filled silent nights even as wars rage and families fight. Do we listen to them because they are part of the background music of the holidays, or because we carry within us a persistent hope that peace really could be born in our hearts, in our families, in our world? Are the melodies of Christmas familiar because we have heard them so often, or because their music was in our first cry?

WHERE IS THE CHILD?

This is a wisdom question that accompanies each of us from birth through life. More existential than physical, it invites us to ponder the geography of our souls all along the way. You and I are each keepers of the question first posed by the Magi of Matthew's gospel: Where is the child? It is not about a shallow quest for the "inner child" of popular psychology. It is the name of the journey drawing us into places not yet explored. Where have I been as I look back in history? What stories of growth and failure, love and loss does my life hold? What experiences have I accrued that make me more compassionate? How truly have I come to know my feelings, my spiritual hungers, and my possibilities? Who knows my heart? What dreams still wait in my soul? We are, each of us, wisdom figures, wise for ourselves and one another. We hold within an unquenchable urge to find holy mystery, to follow its star to the bedside of our most vulnerable selves.

Celebrated as the feast of the Epiphany in the Western church, the visit of the Magi is placed in Matthew's nativity narrative to lead us to the house where the child Jesus is found with Mary, his mother. There are no angels or shepherds, no crowded inns or straw-filled mangers, just travelers like us, following a star. For Matthew, the visitors from the East symbolize the expansion of God's outreach to include those considered outside of it, especially the Gentiles. His Jewish audience has to deal with the implications of Jesus' first guests being foreigners. Not only do the Magi come from outside Jewish or even Gentile circles, but they most likely represent astral religion. "Some early Christians were scandalized at this narrative because of the role of the star."[5] As some Christians today who are very critical of any spirituality that welcomes components of Eastern religions, some early Christians saw a connection to astrology in the star—something they rejected as alien to Christianity.

But Matthew's narrative makes room for the star, allowing this exotic luminary to shine a path toward Jesus, and holds up immigrants from a faraway place as his first guests. That which seems totally outside of accepted religious comfort zones is highlighted, and those who would normally be rejected as magicians and astrologists are welcomed into the house. The Magi, whose exact number is not stated in the scriptures, kneel to pay homage to Jesus. They offer their strange-sounding gifts, leaving us with the task of discerning their symbolic meaning. Then they leave. According to the narrative these are not religious converts who see Jesus and change their spiritual practices. Matthew tells us that they went back to their own country—back to the familiar, back to whatever place had shaped their beliefs and worship. Matthew presents Jesus as one who receives all guests of good will, who, at the outset of his life, welcomes the strangers that he will one day ask us to welcome. The narrative makes no suggestion that these sincere visitors are expected to change their faith, to pledge allegiance to Jesus, or to do anything more than what their journey to this place has already asked of them. Fundamental to the meaning and mission of Jesus is respect—respect for those who are different, acceptance of all whose heritage is not the same as ours, and a gracious welcome to all who sincerely offer the gift of themselves. Gold, frankincense, and myrrh—the unfamiliar is accepted.

Where is the child? The question initiates a spiritual journey for any of us seeking wisdom. For the Magi of Matthew's gospel the search takes them through places both unfamiliar and dangerous. Driven to carry on through unknown terrain, they are guided only by a mysterious light and their own interior trust that a momentous meeting awaits. This time the arduous trek does not disappoint. Overwhelming joy rewards them, however briefly.

The journey of the Magi has all of the elements of any vision quest or spiritual search: Changing light in an otherwise dark sky. Unrelenting persistence toward an uncertain destination. Detours and altered paths. Bewildering dreams. Moments of overpowering joy. Meeting the holy. Offering the gifts of the journey. Going home again—to wherever it is that the inner landscape of our souls calls us.

According to Matthew, Jesus had his very own star, a bright globe in the sky that guided those who wanted to meet him. Stars are glimmers in the darkness, shimmering bits of radiance that draw others forward. The same light that helped the Magi find Jesus is part of a mystery that illuminates all significant relationships. Over the course of our lives many people will come our way, sometimes led by curiosity, sometimes by happenstance. But often, attraction will beckon them, a light inside that is hard to explain—a brightness that can only be followed by those willing to make a journey and offer their gifts. We do the same in relationship to them. As sons and daughters of God we too have our very own star—our personal appeal, our individual influence, our unique way of incarnating the holy. We have gifts to offer. Some of us travel a long way to find the reception that the Magi found.

INCARNATION

The gospels give us yet a third narrative about the coming of Jesus without the elaborate flourishes of Matthew's guiding stars and Luke's singing angels. In a minimalist statement about the meaning of Christmas that begins without a birth account, the author of John's gospel says that Jesus came among us:

> *And the Word became flesh and lived among us,*
> *and we have seen his glory,*
> *the glory as of a father's only son,*
> *full of grace and truth. (Jn 1:14)*

The biblical meaning of the nativity of Jesus is incarnation. The holy took on human flesh, became one of us, like us in all things save the violence that we call sin. The interlinear translation of the NRSV puts it this way:

And the word flesh became and he tented in us,
and we watched the splendor of him,
splendor as only born from father,
full of favor and truth. (Jn 1:14)

For a clearer picture of the mystery that John conveys in the opening chapter of his gospel, it is helpful to look at the original Greek words: The *logos* ("word") became *sarx* ("flesh") and *skenoo* ("tented") among or with or in us. All three words have several possible translations, and each adds nuances to a meditation on the meaning of incarnation:

- The message of God became embodied and lived—"tented"—among human beings.
- The doctrine of what it means to be holy has taken shelter in human skin.
- The story of love has made a home with all the races.
- The eloquence of the divine came to dwell in flesh.
- Divine speech found a tabernacle in all that is physical, earthly, and sensuous.

The more common translation of the Greek *en* is "in," but the word may also be rendered "among" or "with": The holy one of God has entered *into us*, taking up abode inside of humanity. Whether we think of God's word *(logos)* as living among us, dwelling with us, or tenting in us, the imagery is that of intense intimacy. Not only has the very utterance of the holy taken up residence in the midst of humanity, but all that is part of being human is infiltrated with the divine. "Jesus took on our flesh to know every human possibility. Each person's slightly off-kilter mixture of doing and being is not foreign to God."[6]

Incarnation says as much about each of us as it says about God. The holy penetrates humanity not with static divinity, but with an active, creative task—nothing less than transforming the world with compassion. The holy enters into us as a sacred trust, giving humanity custody of the beatitudes, charge over good news eagerly awaited by the poor. Release of captives and freedom for all those who are oppressed is in our collective safekeeping. The consequence of incarnation is that all of us—women and men, young and old, wounded and well, gay and straight—have love built into our very essence. We are meant to find one another irresistible as we move through the world hearing the voices of our brothers and sisters who yearn to feel the holy tenting in their being.

Popular Christian spirituality has often seen incarnation as something God did about two thousand years ago, and then only in Jesus, who made a "temporary stopover" in flesh. Such an understanding acknowledges the continued presence of Jesus in humanity through the Spirit but easily regards a heavenly throne as the real home of the risen One. Christological emphasis has been strong on the divinity of Jesus and more perplexed about his humanity—reticent to assign to him any characteristics that appear too undignified for God. But actual humanity eats and sleeps, laughs and cries, sweats and bathes, gets lonely and discouraged, feels sexually aroused, and fears the unknown. As real human beings we struggle with decisions, usually fall in love, and don't know what tomorrow will bring. Central to being human is being limited—not having all the answers, all the capabilities, or all the experiences of all the people who have ever lived. Did Jesus experience his humanity in these chaotic and restricted ways—or did he slip into divinity now and then, sidestepping what full humanity asks? Faith in incarnation means trusting that Jesus entered every corner of humanity—a humanity that continuously surprised and challenged him. He sought solitude and prayer as he discerned how to incarnate God in his own way, in his own time, and with whatever limitations were his.

In *The Human Being* Walter Wink explores the enigmatic son of man sayings found in the Hebrew and Christian scriptures.[7] He suggests that Jesus is the human being that all of us are called to become and that his incarnational task was to "awaken and empower the Humanchild in others."[8] In John's gospel, according to Wink, incarnation is an archetypal truth that is shared by all human beings, prompting them to also incarnate the living God in their lives.[9] Wink contends that Jesus, as the incarnate God, is not synonymous with God in the sense that he does not represent in his person all of the fullness of God. But over the course of his life, Jesus came to *incarnate* the holy, to become in his humanity the goodness and compassion that is also your task and mine.

In incarnation, the hope of God has reached into the cosmos and taken a chance that the human heart will be receptive to carrying the divine dream toward fulfillment. The Johannine writings see Jesus as one who shared the favor that was part of his identity: "From his fullness we have all received, grace upon grace" (Jn 1:16). Like Jesus, others ought to be able to say of us that we are the expression of God in our humanity. When we move among one another, grace is felt and truth is made more visible. Love is palpable.

THE NATIVITY AS TIMELESS METAPHOR

Nativity is ongoing in the human community and in each person. Birth never ceases as each of us strives to become incarnate. Jesus attempts to explain this in one of the most striking uses of metaphor in the gospels—a metaphor that is misunderstood. It occurs when Nicodemus meets Jesus (Jn 3:3–5). Nicodemus is a Pharisee, a Jewish leader, and is presented as an honest seeker who is in the early stages of understanding the message of Jesus.

In their pointed dialogue Nicodemus comes to Jesus "by night" (Jn 3:2) and acknowledges that Jesus must be a teacher who comes from God because of the signs he has worked. Jesus responds: "I tell you, no one can see the reign of God without being born from above" (Jn 3:3). Nicodemus interprets this statement literally, and questions how anyone can be born after having grown old. "Can one enter a second time into the mother's womb and be born?" (Jn 3:4). Nicodemus knows only of births that involve the emergence of babies from mother's wombs—births that provide lineage as well as physical life. But Jesus is talking about a different kind of birth. Being born of flesh gives physical life and makes one a member of a particular people. Birth of the Spirit, on the other hand, brings about an entirely new set of relationships that explode beyond the narrow confines of bloodline. Being born of the Spirit shatters old notions of heritage and makes everyone brothers and sisters. "The Johannine Jesus, then, is radically replacing what constitutes the children of God, challenging any privileged status stemming from natural parenthood."[10] It is not physical ancestry that makes a person part of the family of God, but rather, being born anew. Is this why there is no earthly royalty in Jesus? In an unredeemed way of thinking, Mary and Joseph were certainly not suitable parents for a child of God. But in God's way of thinking, they were the perfect pair: Ordinary. Average people are good enough to parent the sons and daughters of God.

What does it mean to be born again? Most obviously a reference to Christian baptism, the phrase has implications beyond a single sacramental ritual. Being born again means *living* our baptism—being born again, and again, and again in love: "Beloved, let us love one another, because love is from God; everyone who loves is born of God and knows God" (1 Jn 4:7). The author of the first letter of John is emphatic about the significance of love, manifested in service, as the primary sign of birth in the Spirit: "We know love by this, that he laid down his life for us—and we ought to lay down our lives for one another" (1 Jn 3:16).

Many Christians have understood the born-again metaphor as literally as did Nicodemus. They have taken it to mean a dramatic experience that gives them privileged status among God's sons and daughters—exactly the opposite of what Jesus is trying to teach Nicodemus. Being born again is not defined by a single occurrence in which I accept Jesus as Lord, particularly if this means a theatrical spectacle followed by an elitist rejection of all those who have not been part of an extraordinary conversion experience. Being born again does not involve reliving one's first birth or staging a second one. It is a process rather than a moment. It occurs every time you and I lay down our lives in quiet care for others. In this sense, being born again gives timeless endurance to the incarnation of Jesus.

The mystery of the nativity is that love is made incarnate every time it deepens in us. As we grow in love, we give birth to loving acts. We make love more present in the world. As Christmas is born again in each of us, it comes forth again into the world. We are called to be birth givers—those who, like Mary, give birth in the most unexpected places.

EVERYDAY NATIVITY

The nativity of Jesus cannot be tucked away in a stable in Bethlehem or laid in a manger behind a crowded inn. It isn't a box of decorations to unpack once a year, nor is it a seasonal story to read to children under the Christmas tree. The birth of every child is a holy nativity, good news of great joy deserving of a heavenly host praising God and singing, "Glory to God in the highest heaven" (Lk 2:14). Each time a child is born, we hear again the voice of angels proclaiming peace on earth, reminding us of the kind of world every newborn baby needs in order to grow into the fullness of grace and truth that the nativity of Jesus announces. In Italian, *dare alla luce* means to give birth—literally, "to give to the light." The phrase describes what every birth ought to mean, that an infant is given over to the light, surrounded by every opportunity to grow, to shine, to illuminate love.

The deepest message of nativity is not about physical birth. It is about transformation toward love in those already born. Incarnation of the holy happens whenever we act justly, love tenderly, and walk in truth with our God. Sometimes it develops slowly, when we consciously set out on the long journey toward integrity and honor that commitment over the course of our lives. Other times an opportunity for giving birth comes upon us when we least expect it, when we are ill prepared for the demands of love that rise up in front of us—an apology is called for, a truth needs to be announced, words of forgiveness must be spoken, affirmation is needed.

It is true that larger missions await, those that affect the globe, turning it in the direction of justice—into a world where the wolf lives with the lamb and the lion and ox share food, and have enough. But it is often the quiet, small actions that make love more available to those who stand next to me, who live in my house, work in my building, and drive on the same roads that I do. Bringing forth life is neither gender specific nor age restricted. Giving birth is bringing new energy into a weary situation. It involves the hard labor of pushing away hindrances that stifle people, keeping them in spaces too small for their dreams. The Carmelite Sisters of Reno publish a card that reads: "What you do with your heart affects the whole universe." It is true; one heartbeat can reproduce love in a second.

The nativity narratives of Matthew and Luke remind us that we can expect days when there will be no room for us in the inns of other people's hearts, times when the journey feels unfair or too arduous, times when we have lost our way. These hurdles can mean that we have to make the best of situations not to our liking, to keep going because there is no turning back. Other times they might be signposts alerting us to danger, urging us to take a different route—like the Magi, we are warned to end a dubious relationship and find another way home. But every once in a while, discomforts and complications serve as notice that we are nearing Bethlehem, where a sacred birth is imminent.

"Fran, Cassandra and I are at the hospital. The doctor said we'll have our little girl before the end of the day!" My nephew Darin spoke softly, almost in a whisper, as though he were standing in the sanctuary of a great cathedral. His voice held excitement and calm together as well as any first-time father could. He had called on my cell phone as I drove home from the Portland airport. The instant I heard his greeting, something leaped within me—good news of great joy often has that effect. I got to the hospital within the hour. There, those of us gathered in vigil hugged and welcomed tears of early joy. As the hours went by, we talked of this baby girl's meaning in our joined families. Like the children of Mary and Elizabeth, indeed each newborn, this child would be unique. As a daughter of the God who created women and men in the image of the holy, she would bring a new sacred portrait to the earth. She would have her own special call, her gifts, and her way of moving through the world with a blessing.

In the process she will become another holy nativity, incarnation once again. For her, and for each of us, the day of her birth is just the beginning of the call to incarnate the holy God whose first creative action was to give birth to the universe.

Ashlee Jae arrived later that evening. Angels sang to welcome her.

Chapter 5

Baptism

Plunging into Life

> *In those days Jesus came from Nazareth of Galilee*
> *and was baptized by John in the Jordan.*
> *And just as he was coming up out of the water,*
> *he saw the heavens torn apart*
> *and the Spirit descending like a dove on him.*
> *And a voice came from heaven,*
> *"You are my Son, the Beloved;*
> *with you I am well pleased." (Mk 1:9–11)*

> *Then Jesus came from Galilee to John at the Jordan,*
> *to be baptized by him.*
> *John would have prevented him, saying,*
> *"I need to be baptized by you, and do you come to me?"*
> *But Jesus answered him,*
> *"Let it be so now; for it is proper for us in this way to fulfill all*
> *righteousness."*
> *Then he consented.*
> *And when Jesus had been baptized,*
> *just as he came up from the water,*
> *suddenly the heavens were opened to him*
> *and he saw the Spirit of God*
> *descending like a dove and alighting on him.*
> *And a voice from heaven said,*

"This is my Son, the Beloved,
with whom I am well pleased." (Mt 3:13–17)

Now when all the people were baptized,
and when Jesus also had been baptized and was praying,
the heaven was opened,
and the Holy Spirit descended upon him
in bodily form like a dove.
And a voice came from heaven,
"You are my Son, the Beloved;
with you I am well pleased." (Lk 3:21–22)

And John testified,
"I saw the Spirit descending from heaven like a dove,
and it remained on him. I myself did not know him,
but the one who sent me to baptize with water said to me,
'He on whom you see the Spirit descend and remain
is the one who baptizes with the Holy Spirit.'" (Jn 1:32–33)

BAPTIZING SAMMY

He was dressed all in white, with a temperament as bright as his outfit. When his father gently held him over the fount, and water was poured on his head, he smacked his lips and smiled. Once again, an ancient ritual that Jesus underwent in the Jordan was celebrated. Sammy was baptized.

But he was not quite as acquiescent when the baptismal garment, symbolic of being clothed in Christ, was placed on his chest. As the priest prayed the words reminding him, and all of us, of the responsibilities of baptism, Sammy, in one quick clench of his tiny fist, grabbed the garment and flung it to the ground. As the gasps of his two older brothers, Cole and Miles, turned to giggles, Sammy clapped his hands. Did his deft gesture embody an unconscious sense that baptism has implications that cannot be imposed? His parents, Sean and Megan, had carried him into the church, but little Sammy will have to make the journey required of a disciple himself. He will need to learn to dress his soul in his baptism, picking up the dispositions of love and wearing them as comfortably as an old shirt. It will take his entire life.

PLUNGING IN

Baptizo. The Greek word means "dip," "plunge," or "wash with water." Water washings described in the Hebrew bible initially represent ritual ablutions related to sacrifice and Temple observance (Lv 16:4, 24). In later writings these purification rites gradually become connected to actions in behalf of justice:

> *Wash yourselves; make yourselves clean;*
> *remove the evil of your doings*
> *from before my eyes; cease to do evil, learn to do good;*
> *seek justice, rescue the oppressed,*
> *defend the orphan, plead for the widow. (Is 1:16–17)*

In Jeremiah the water ritual assumes a clear metaphorical tone: "O Jerusalem, wash your heart clean of wickedness" (Jer 4:14). The people are urged to undergo an interior cleansing, removing evil intentions and sinfulness from their hearts. Ezekiel expands this notion in one of the bible's most poetic descriptions of the effects of ritual washing:

> *I will sprinkle clean water upon you,*
> *and you shall be clean*
> *from all your uncleannesses,*
> *and from all your idols I will cleanse you.*
> *A new heart I will give you,*
> *and a new spirit I will put within you;*
> *and I will remove from your body the heart of stone*
> *and give you a heart of flesh. (Ez 36:25)*

For these prophets, uncleanness is associated with ritual impurity, with a failure to honor the obligations imposed by the law of holiness outlined for all of the people in the book of Leviticus (Lv 17—26). Concerned largely with dietary rules, sexual restrictions, idolatry, and various prohibitions, Leviticus connects holiness with practices considered acceptable or "clean." In the early writings cleanness was understood literally. In Israel's development as a people, strict observance of these distinct behaviors helped them recognize themselves as a group and maintain an identity that was separate from their Canaanite neighbors. Ironically, practices that confirmed separation *from others* would one day be reversed, evolving into rituals that proclaim just the opposite: All that God has created is clean. Everyone belongs.

As prophetic voices challenge the people to cleanse themselves on the inside, superficial washings evolve into spiritual experiences with serious implications. Sprinkling with water is an exterior symbol of something deeper. Israel is called to replace callous attitudes and claims of privilege with care for those in need. Reaching out to the oppressed and welcoming those who have no community are signs that the rituals are taking effect in the hearts of the people. A new spirit of compassion becomes the essence of authentic religious experience. For the followers of Jesus, it is a message we are still struggling to learn.

I still have my baptismal garment, yellowed and threadbare now. For much of my early life I had no idea that this sacrament had committed me to far-reaching actions of justice. When I first learned about my baptism, I was told that it had saved me from a forbidding place called limbo had I died before its rescuing waters had been poured over my infant head. Decades later I would learn that the opposite was true: Instead of rescuing *me*, my baptism obligates me to *liberate others*. Baptism had put in me a new spirit and replaced what could become a heart of stone with a heart of flesh. Little had I known that this ritual dunking would implant in me a compulsion to rescue the oppressed, defend the orphan, and plead for the widow! At least, that is how it is supposed to work when ancient water rituals give way to communal sacraments in which parents, sponsors, and entire faith communities promise to help us live our baptismal commitments. What do you know about your baptism? How often do you revisit the implications of this first sacramental moment in your life? What has it propelled you toward?

Plunging in can take many forms, each of them a manifestation of the baptismal force within. I plunge into life whenever I let go of crutches and dependencies, protections I no longer need or things that hold me back from being the person that I am called to be. I plunge in when I choose to leave home for the first time, to go to school, to get a job, to strike out on my own—to go anywhere or do anything simply because it is time, without any assurance that it will be successful. There is something unnerving about a true baptismal plunge. For a moment after my feet have left the ground I am airborne! My security is gone. I am making my way down the jetway of a plane that will transport me to an unfamiliar place. I am signing a contract that commits me to a lifelong relationship. I have entered a treatment center where I will have to relinquish my self-destructive patterns. I am moving into a retirement home wondering where the years have gone. I can no longer lean on comforts that have become familiar or events that I can predict in my sleep. I am plunging in because I must, because it is right, because my baptismal energy is whispering in my soul.

"A trip to Nicaragua was organized at my office to provide two weeks of dental care. I wanted to go but I was apprehensive. Could I handle the conditions? I prayed about it and finally found the courage to roll up my sleeves and go for it." This man's description of plunging in for the sake of others was a genuine baptismal leap. Such a step involves overcoming inner resistance, often the fear of the unknown, and setting out, making a commitment, getting something done that needs doing for the human community. In this sense Christian baptism is a dive into the reign of God, immersion in the mystery of incarnating the holy.

JOHN THE BAPTIZER

In the Christian community formal baptism with water is introduced with John, called the Baptist. The son of Elizabeth and Zechariah, "the hand of the Lord was with him" (Lk 1:66), and he "grew and became strong in spirit, and he was in the wilderness until the day he appeared publicly to Israel" (Lk 1:80). This description is as much about you and me as it is about John the Baptist. The hand of the holy accompanies us—a biblical metaphor of God's steadfast presence. With this ever-present, guiding hand, we grow and, it is to be hoped, become strong in spirit, gradually confirmed in our beliefs and committed to living them. The Greek word *krataioo* ("strengthen") implies a process—a slow, ongoing deepening that readies each of us to enter our particular wilderness, perhaps many times. Whether referencing John the Baptist, Jesus, or any one of us, becoming strong in spirit commits us to a baptismal plunge into human wholeness, into full immersion into the life circumstances that are uniquely our own.

Baptism is neither a reckless dive nor a casual one. My best baptismal decisions are made carefully and intentionally. I choose to learn to communicate more effectively, to listen with greater concentration to those I love. I decide to accept feedback from a friend without becoming defensive—a true plunge into healthy vulnerability. I commit myself to exploring my feelings instead of ignoring them, and I am met with humble awareness.

According to Luke, John the Baptist first encounters Jesus while surrounded by the most sacred of waters, the amniotic fluid of his mother's womb. The effect of that primal baptism never left him. Like his mother, who had exclaimed with a loud cry of recognition when Mary entered the house, pregnant with Jesus, John also announces Mary's son (Lk 1:42). By the time we meet John as an adult, his silent leap in the nativity narrative has matured into a bold proclamation of faith. That is the way of baptism, indeed any ritual. When it is genuine, it has consequences. It expands from a singular, often quiet experience to a raging energy that cannot be stilled. Now, a wild-looking man who appears out of the desert, John is presented as a herald once again, as one whose lifelong destiny is to point to Jesus. His precocious leap of awareness in the womb of Elizabeth now has a voice (Lk 1:44).

While all four evangelists connect John to "the voice" that Isaiah foretold, it is only in the fourth gospel that the Baptist directly claims this voice as his own: "I am the voice of one crying

out in the wilderness, 'Make straight the way of the Lord,' as the
prophet Isaiah said" (Jn 1:23). John has certainty about who he
is and proclaims the message of his convictions without self-
aggrandizement: "I baptize with water. Among you stands one
whom you do not know, the one who is coming after me; I am
not worthy to untie the thong of his sandal" (Jn 1:26–27). Although his message carries a sense of urgency and fervor is in his
voice, John's time of ministry is brief. His recorded words are
few. In all of the gospels he serves to call attention to Jesus, and
then he fades from the scene, as he indicates he must: "He must
increase, but I must decrease" (Jn 3:30).

Although the words could sound self-deprecating to the psy-
chologically attuned ear, John's was not a ministry born of low
self-esteem. When I promote others with true sincerity I need
healthy self-confidence to step aside without feeling resentful or
diminished. Perhaps one of the most loving things any of us can
do is to highlight others, promote their shining, and experience
true joy in the process: "The friend of the bridegroom, who stands
and hears him, rejoices greatly at the bridegroom's voice. For
this reason, my joy has been fulfilled" (Jn 3:29). Using biblical
imagery and words somewhat foreign to contemporary hearers,
John the Baptist comes to us as a person who has internalized the
effects of the baptism he practiced. He has claimed his own voice
and uses it with courage. He wants others to come to know Jesus
and to live his message. He is willing to see his own importance
decline as this happens. He teaches out of his abundant passion,
then stands aside. It is what great teachers do. It is how the best
parents prepare their children for life. It is what friends do when
they offer their deeply held convictions yet respect the freedom
of the other to think differently.

I AM A VOICE

The fourth gospel uses the voice of John the Baptist as a witness
to Jesus, to testify strongly and surely that he is the Son of God:
"And I myself have seen and have testified that this is the Son of

God (Jn 1:34). These words were intended to convince the hearers of John's gospel that Jesus was real. The Baptist was convincing. The synoptic gospels tell us that people flocked to the water to be baptized by John. The strict and exacting God that John preached was alluring to those who were familiar with a God whose standards for them were often out of reach. Perhaps they were driven to the river out of a sense of unworthiness, a collective guilt that sought relief. Then, as today, it can be easier to believe in a God who is annoyed with us than one who finds us lovable.

For John, baptism is a call to repentance, an exhortation to abandon sinful ways in order to appease an angry God (Mk 1:4). His is a traditional water ritual, a symbolic washing meant to shake the people into awareness about how they live their lives. All the evangelists are careful to distinguish John's baptism from that of Jesus:

> *I baptize you with water;*
> *but he will baptize you with the Holy Spirit. (Lk 3:16)*

But even John's baptism has implications. More than just a ceremony in the Jordan that forgives sin, like the water rites of the Hebrew writings, John's baptism requires a change of heart. He is blunt when the people asked him what they need to do: Share your resources with those who most need them. Be honest and fair in your dealings with others. Be satisfied with what you have earned (Lk 3:10–14). He echoes earlier prophets: Act justly. Love tenderly. Walk humbly with your God (Mi 6:8). Without these accompanying behaviors John's baptism would have been another empty ritual—comforting in the moment, perhaps, but devoid of any lasting consequence. Like any sacrament today, the grace of the event needs to be a source of strengthening, an impetus that makes us more alive and more compassionate. Otherwise, it can easily devolve into little more than a dunk in a river, leaving us wet but not prophetic.

A significant consequence of John's form of baptism is highlighted by Luke, who alone quotes the Isaian prophecy more extensively: "All flesh shall see the salvation of God" (Lk 3:6). Not only is a voice crying out in the wilderness to prepare for the way of the Lord, but, in the fuller words of Isaiah:

> *Then the glory of the Lord shall be revealed,*
> *And all people shall see it together. (Is 40:5)*

Although Luke expands the quotation from Isaiah to make sure that his Gentile audience feels included, his theological concern is prophetic. God's dream is inclusivity, an expansive embrace of everyone. The Lucan John the Baptist reaches out to "all flesh"—to everyone who is excluded, marginalized, and left out. His is both a voice and a vision. It cries out to remind us that the true way of the Lord is a way that invites in, rather than shuts out, a way that opens up possibilities instead of closing doors. It is a voice that prepares the way for round tables and big tents, a vision for all the people to see together. With Lucan baptismal theology, a scattered and disconnected populace flocks to the river and is baptized. A community emerges from the water.

I am a voice. John the Baptist is a symbol of every baptized Christian, one called to come out of the background places of life and behave in a manner that calls attention to Jesus. Perhaps one of the first steps of this adult baptismal process is to know the sound of my own voice, and to claim that which is most authentically baptismal in it. My voice has a baptismal commission: to speak truth, to promote justice, to give visibility to healthy communication.

I am a voice—or am I? Have I ever remained silent in the face of injustice out of fear, uncertainty, or a belief that I have more important things to do? Busyness, daily distractions, and genuine obligations can stifle my baptismal voice or dull its urgency. A tendency to avoid conflict can keep my baptismal voice from being audible. Maybe next week I will have more time to call my senator about health care for all. Once I read more about it, I will bring up the subject of sex trafficking in a conversation. Even closer to home—perhaps that apology gnawing away in the back of my throat can wait. I will speak my needs later or encourage my child tomorrow. I don't want to say anything that will embarrass anyone, so I will refrain from objecting to gossip. A common avoidance of holy speech is rooted in a belief that someone else will say what needs to be said, and probably articulate it better. While it is important to discern the opportune moment to speak, there is really no excuse for silencing my voice of justice. My words of compassion will have no impact if they are swallowed. The way of the Lord is always in need of a fresh voice—quite possibly, mine!

If, like John the Baptist, I am a voice, it is important that I examine its tone and content. What kind of voice do I offer to the world, to my family, my place of work, my ministry? There are disgruntled voices, whiny voices, critical voices, none of which put baptismal energy into the air. The voice of baptism is characterized by truth interwoven with compassion. The baptismal voice is prophetic, calling for an end to oppression and an increase of love. Like the Baptist, prophetic voices are often called to speak out when no one else is doing so. Not infrequently, their message is unpopular: End the war. Empower the poor. Welcome the immigrant. Let's talk to each other. Like any of us who are hesitant to speak out, early prophets had to face their inner resistance. Who would not be at least a little reluctant to speak for God—perhaps alone a sign of the prophet's authenticity?

The call to use my voice in behalf of justice can seem mysterious, bewildering in its persistence or discomforting in its intensity, but it is not an exceptional call. It is ordinary. Being a voice for right and goodness is in the water, the baptismal water. Once I have been to the river, dipped in the living waters of baptism, making straight the way is my destiny. Like John, I am called to come out of the unobtrusive places and say, "I am a voice." I am a voice sent to remind, annoy, and pester in behalf of justice. I am a voice sent to comfort, to heal, to teach. I am a voice sent to disturb the complacent and soothe the brokenhearted. Mine is a voice never to be silenced until the voices of all of my brothers and sisters have a chance to speak.

A SPIRIT LIKE A DOVE

All the gospels report that the baptism of Jesus was accompanied by a theophany, a visible manifestation of the Spirit in the form of a dove. In Mark and Matthew it occurs just as Jesus is coming up out of the water. In Luke it happens after the baptismal event, while Jesus is at prayer. In John's gospel the emphasis is on the Baptist's recognition and witness that Jesus is the Son of God (Jn 1:32).

Jung noticed that images of Spirit abound in scripture—the *ruah* (wind/spirit/breath) of Genesis 1 being the most familiar. To Jung, all of them are God images. Modern-day biblical scholars would not disagree. When the Spirit descends as a dove upon Jesus at his baptism, we instinctively know that it *represents* God, but that God is not a dove. We are invited to ponder this biblical image, while keeping it symbolic—because it holds a hint of what God is like.

So, how is God like a dove? The dove image, having its source in an early tradition, has been more enduring than any other symbolic representation of the Spirit of God. The image is prolific in religious art, jewelry, and sculpture. Almost synonymous with the Holy Spirit in the minds of many, the dove symbol penetrates deeply into inherited patterns of primal meaning that dwell in the human unconscious.

How did this particular image come to those who associated the baptism of Jesus with a manifestation of the Spirit of God? Similar to the powerful recollections carried by any one of us regarding a momentous event, memory of a strong spiritual experience associated with the baptism of Jesus likely circulated among the people. In time, this memory evolved into an oral tradition as it was told and retold. It became a story of faith, one designed to elicit belief that the Spirit of God was with Jesus in a palpable way. The presence of the Spirit was connected to his baptism. It was real. And to convey its genuineness over time, and assist in its retelling, a symbol was associated with the story. The tradition of the descent of the dove on Jesus, inherited by the evangelists, *resonated* with each of them. It sounded a tone of familiarity in their individual minds and *inspired* them sufficiently to include it in their gospels. According to Robert J. Karris, "The dove symbolized the hopes of men and women for love, life, and union with God," hopes now realized in Jesus.[1]

Symbols and images function to solidify memories of notable events. We are more apt to recall significant events if we can picture them in our minds. A symbol, like a dove, conveys the gentle innocence of God's tender care. While the dove symbol might have been influenced by other examples of God's hovering presence in the Hebrew writings, it had to capture the interest of the evangelists to remain connected to the baptismal story.

Matthew's Jesus, amid instruction to go to the lost sheep of Israel to proclaim the good news, cautions the Twelve: "See, I am sending you out like sheep into the midst of wolves; so be wise as serpents and innocent as doves" (Mt 10:16).

Sheep and wolves. Serpents and doves. Wisdom and innocence. The pairings represent a masterful weaving of symbolic language in the gospel. When the wisdom accorded the serpent is linked to the innocence of the dove, the mandate for discipleship is evocative. Jesus uses these figurative symbols to remind his disciples what they will be facing as they negotiate life. They are reminders to each of us as well: Be aware. Be watchful. Rely on your powers of perception. Look deeply into things. Remember what you have learned from experience. And, in the process, retain your baptismal innocence. As disciples, you and I are to run through the world with innocent wisdom—insightful enough to do no harm, and secure enough to trust the inner knowing residing in our hearts.

In another use of the dove image in scripture, Jesus finds people selling animals in the Temple. The story is told in one form or another by all the evangelists, though Luke does not mention the doves:

> *In the temple, he found people selling cattle, sheep, and doves,*
> *and the money changers seated at their tables.*
> *Making a whip of cords, he drove all of them out of the temple,*

both the sheep and the cattle.
He also poured out the coins of the money changers
and overturned their tables.
He told those who were selling the doves,
"Take these things out of here!
Stop making my Father's house a marketplace!" (Jn 2:14–16)

It was customary for moneychangers to sit in the Temple area, changing Greek and Roman money into the coins pilgrims needed to buy sacrificial animals. The dove was the typical sacrifice for women, lepers, and the poor (Lv 12:6–8; 14:22). In a display of anger unusual for Jesus in the Christian writings, he drives out the animals and their sellers and upsets the tables of the moneychangers. In John's gospel he turns to those selling the doves and addresses them without doing them violence. "Take these things out of here!"

The narrative is familiar as the cleansing of the Temple. Placed at the beginning of John's gospel, with related reference to the temple that is Jesus' body, it is one of the many signs that John uses to establish Jesus' true identity. In addition to its messianic symbolism it offers an image of cleansing in which a river of angst purifies the elements of abuse and injustice that have crept into temple sacrifice. In Jesus, anger becomes power for renewal, a baptismal energy that enables him to act for justice. The Temple's plunge into these holy waters is designed to wash it of corruption, restore its integrity. Anything that represents injustice, that promotes that subjugation of the poor, is removed from the Temple. Restored to its original purpose, it is a house of the holy where women and men find a God who is accessible to all.

"Take these things out of here!" Temple sacrifice aimed at financial gain at the expense of the poor has come to an end. After this ritual baptism, women and lepers can come into God's house without cost. And the lowly dove—its cage is opened. No longer a symbol of bartering for God's favor that only the poor can afford, it is released to fly free.

What about those of us who believe that we are *temples of the holy*—embodied residences where God's goodness is supposed to find receptive dwelling? How do we hear these words—"take these things out of here"? Is there anything in *my temple* that ought to be removed because it inhibits the approach to God's graciousness? Is there any jealousy, any selfishness, or any bullying? What do I require of people who seek admittance to my respect? Are there obligations that others incur in exchange for my kindness to them? Who has access, and who does not?

SYMBOL AND THE QUEST FOR WISDOM

The early community, through John the Baptist, held that Jesus would baptize with the Holy Spirit and fire (Mt 3:11). While the meaning of that phrase is obscure, fire often serves as a metaphor for intense arousal—like the type that consumes Jesus. The anger he displays in the Temple is fire for his mission. In the face of injustice, anger can be a powerful source of energy to confront many forms of oppression. My anger can be fire in the service of the holy. It can put intensity into my voice and strengthen my resolve to fight discrimination and unfairness wherever I see them.

To the extent that I am a serious disciple, the Holy Spirit and fire are symbols that can neither be separated from each other nor disengaged from my interior life. If I lack holy wisdom, my "fire" can quickly turn into a caldron of misdirected rage, exploding into caustic tantrums that do nothing to restore justice for the oppressed. Inappropriately expressed anger, however justified it might seem at the time, can become just another source of oppression for people in my life. But without any "fire," if compassion is absent from my heart, my insights, however lofty, will not provide a launching pad to further ignite the reign of God. I will be one more dour person, more pious than prophetic.

Achieving fiery wisdom involves plumbing my reservoir of knowledge, born of life experience, and reflecting deeply about how I express it. Such passionate awareness does not come to me from books written by others or rules imposed from outside. I will not come to prophetic knowing only by conforming to external mandates. True wisdom is baptismal knowledge—it is what we know from plunging into life, remembering what we have experienced, and listening to others who have made a similar journey.

For Jung, "wisdom is a return" to archetypal symbols.[2] There exists in us an internal stream of intuitive knowing that is not in our conscious awareness. Paying attention to symbols, images, and dreams lights a path, helping us know what we know and see what we see. Matthew presents Joseph, Mary's husband and the father of Jesus, as a man who looked inward, who was particularly responsive to his inner sense of things (Mt 1:20–24; 2:13–15). Attuned to his dreams, his keen perceptions become angels, messengers that guide his way and create a future for those he loves. My dreams might do the same for me and for my loved ones. At the very least, I can examine them for clues about facets of my life that feel safe enough to come out only in the stillness of the night.

A VOICE FROM HEAVEN

In all three synoptic gospels the descent of the dove is accompanied by a *voice from heaven*. In Mark and Luke the voice speaks directly to Jesus. In Matthew it addresses other hearers declaring the true nature of Jesus: "You are my Son, my Beloved." Although the voice and dove images are united in the same theophany, the dove is not the source of the voice. We are told that the voice is coming from heaven.

Occurring about three hundred times in the Christian scriptures, the Greek *ouranos* (almost always translated "heaven," but also meaning "air" and "sky") is obscure in origin. Related to the Greek *anemos* (meaning "wind"), the notions of breath, wind, spirit, and life are intimately connected grammatically. *Anemos* is the source of both *animate* and *animal* ("one that breathes"). The ambiguous *ouranos* expresses the human struggle to locate the holy, to give it tangibility. But wandering through our many languages, seeking a glimpse of God's dwelling, inevitably leads to the conclusion that heaven is not a place "up there" or "out there" as much as it is a metaphor for the *way* of God. In that sense *heaven* is that home of the holy that is at once *everywhere* and *nowhere*. It is the unimpeded spirit of love moving about, like wind, flooding the heart with compassion that spills over into actions that proclaim all are one, all have a right to inhabit the earth, and all are cherished.

A voice from heaven is an inner voice, the *anima* and *animus* movement of all-enveloping love within you, within me, that has its origin in God. From a theological perspective the heavenly voice in the baptismal scene confirms for all the people not only that Jesus is God's son, but that he is utterly and totally loved by the holy one he called Abba. Looking at the scene from the lens of psychology, the voice from heaven represents what Jung would call an "archetypal drama of the Self."[3] It is Jesus coming to adult awareness that he is lovable—not for what he has accomplished, or whom he has impressed, but simply because he is, like each of us, a child of the holy. This uneducated, socially marginal, obscure peasant learns that his value lies not in the ways that societies the world over usually define it. He comes to know, from deep within his humanness, that he is good, that he incarnates the holy. In much the same way, each of us listens for a voice from heaven prompting the same soaring awareness in our lives.

Do you ever feel insignificant? Does it seem that you don't have enough education, social standing, or a resume that compares to that of others? Is your list of failures longer than your page of accomplishments? Has your family been disappointed in you? At the same time, do you honestly try to listen for the voice of God in your life—to be a good person, to do your best given your gifts and limitations? Do you fail, sometimes even with that? Then the voice that Jesus heard in his life is speaking the same message to you: You are dear to me. I see a parent's reflection in your every movement. You are my daughter, my son; you are part of a vast universe of love.

Many of the most endearing stories are those of people coming to greater self-awareness. In *The Color Purple* there is a scene where the main character, Celie, finally claims her dignity. In the film version of the book the entire family is gathered around a

Thanksgiving table. After continuously being taunted by her abusive husband, Celie grabs a large carving knife and ominously suspends it in the air over him. In a gripping clash between the internal forces of good and evil, she finally stabs the knife into the table with such force that its handle vibrates back and forth for several seconds. As everyone exhales, Celie proclaims: "I'm pore, I'm black, I may be ugly and can't cook. . . . But I'm here."[4] In a single noble movement she averts the destructive temptation within and asserts her true worth. It is a baptismal moment.

Not all baptism takes place in rivers and founts. Baptism is that split second when we know what Jesus knew at the edge of the Jordan, what Celie came to understand out of the desolation of her life: There is love in us that has its source in the holy. We can be struggling. Our personal history might hold a lifetime of mistakes, or a spirit that has been crushed. Like Jesus at the time of his river experience, we might be unknown and unaccomplished. But there is love in us. And we are here!

Baptism comes differently to each of us. Before or after a sacrament that pours water over our heads, we are confronted with baptismal opportunities. They are offers to go deeper, to choose right over wrong, truth over evasion. But the primary thrust of baptism is to hear an inner voice saying that we are beloved— and believing it.

It is easy to over-spiritualize the stories of Jesus, to think of them happening only to him. But his coming to personalized awareness of love is also our task. Paul reminds us that God says the same thing to each of us: "As God's chosen ones, holy and beloved, clothe yourselves with compassion, kindness, humility, meekness, and patience" (Col 3:12). The word that Paul uses to describe God's love for each of us (*agapao*) is the same used to describe God's love for Jesus at his baptism (*agapetos*). The word, from *agape*, means "very dear" or "beloved." It is especially prevalent in all of the Pauline writings; those who have been baptized are continually called beloved of God. Descriptive of baptismal relationship, approaching one another as *beloved*, creating experiences of *belovedness* for one another ought to be part of our intentional way of expressing our baptism. Clothe yourselves, Paul says, using the characteristics of love as a metaphorical garment.

Wrap yourselves in truth, wear kindness everywhere, and put on compassion like a cloak. Make all of these things so much a part of your life that you would feel naked without them.

A BAPTISM TO UNDERGO

Baptism is a sacramental water ritual that claims us as members of a community of believers. But like so many biblical signs and rituals, its meaning cannot be fully expressed in a single image. Baptism involves water but it starts a fire. Jesus employs a metaphorical understanding of baptism when he says: "I come to bring fire to the earth, and how I wish it were already kindled! I have a baptism with which to be baptized, and what stress I am under until it is completed" (Lk 12:49–50). Wink speaks of these words as containing the "original impulse" of Jesus.[5] For Jesus, baptism was under his skin. An *impulse* had been ignited in him that could not be extinguished. Enkindling this fire was the thrust of his life. The cooling waters of the Jordan gave him a message of love, but there was another baptism that would burn him.

That is the way of baptism, for Jesus and for each of us. We celebrate a ritual with family and friends and then plunge into the harsh places of life. Over time, passion builds that will not be quenched, if we are paying attention. Often it is a little fire with a big dream, a spark seeking to be part of a larger blaze that fans the message of God's reign far and wide. Our personal baptismal journey is a task that will agitate us until it is undertaken.

Workshops are conducted and books are written to help people *find their passion*. While such a phrase can be a cliché, the search for one's passion is a serious one—especially baptismal passion. Have you found yours? What is it that burns inside of you, wanting more oxygen, seeking to grow? The scope of your passion is less important than its presence. Whether a diminutive ember or a massive blaze, its purpose is to warm your soul, to fire your commitment to a life immersed in goodness. Perhaps it is parenting or teaching. It might be creating with your hands or your imagination or your voice. It could be working for a social justice cause or pursuing a personal dream on which time is running out, as with a friend of mine:

> *My younger brother is severely autistic. He still faces daily hurdles that I don't have. If hearts can be broken, mine was in pieces throughout my childhood. I ached for him. All my life I dreamed of doing something to help but I didn't know what it might be. Then, after my own two children started school, I plunged in: I tried to get into graduate school, but didn't make it. I didn't give up. I didn't leave a single stone unturned. Now I am assisting a medical team working on autism research. It feels like I have finally found my deeper calling. Just last week my brother, who is nearly forty and still has trouble speaking, said, "I love you, Sis." His words felt as though they were coming from God.*

Perhaps they were.

Chapter 6

Temptation

Choices in the Wilderness

And the Spirit immediately drove him out into the wilderness.
He was in the wilderness for forty days, tempted by Satan;
and he was with the wild beasts;
and the angels waited on him. (Mk 1:12–13)

Then Jesus was led up by the Spirit into the wilderness
to be tempted by the devil.
He fasted forty days and forty nights,
and afterwards he was famished.
The tempter came and said to him,
"If you are the Son of God, . . . " (Mt 4:1–3)

Jesus, full of the Holy Spirit, returned from the Jordan
and was led by the Spirit in the wilderness,
where for forty days he was tempted by the devil.
He ate nothing at all during those days, and when they were over,
he was famished. The devil said to him,
"If you are the Son of God, . . . (Lk 4:1–3)

LED TO THE UNFAMILIAR

I remember those days as clearly as yesterday, though it has been
decades since I flew alone from Oregon to Wisconsin to enter

the convent. Everything from the food to the early September humidity felt alien. As the wilderness of this strange new place closed in around me, I was tempted to ease my loneliness in so many ways: "You can make secret phone calls home," the voice in my head whispered. "There is a flight out of here tomorrow— your parents will come to meet you at the Portland airport," it said. "Eat more homemade bread with peanut butter and you will feel better," it promised. Whether *led* or *driven* here I still don't know. It was something that was inside me to do.

Being filled with the Spirit of holiness did not eliminate ordinary burdens of life for Jesus, and it won't eliminate them for us. The wilderness, in some form, can summon us any time. While Matthew, Mark, and Luke write slightly different accounts of the wilderness ordeal, each understands that Jesus faces trials as he honors the truth of his life. Like the Israelites who encounter obstacles during the Exodus, Jesus' sojourn of forty days in the wilderness recalls the forty years of wandering of his ancestors— only he responds without grumbling and complaining. "His response to Israel's key temptations, however, contrasts with that of Israel and finally fulfills the latter's vocation."[1]

The wilderness narrative clarifies who Jesus is, and who he is not. The powerful story confronts the dominant expectation that God would send a descendant of David to become the future king who would occupy the throne of Israel (Jer 33:15). Although the identity of such a messiah or anointed one remains vague in the Hebrew literature, there was a popular sense that his reign would be political.

Walter Wink, like other biblical scholars, contends that Jesus was continually faced with rejecting the three leading roles that were associated with the coming of the messiah: prophet, priest, and king. Even though the church later assigned each of these roles to Jesus, Wink notes that an early branch of Christianity "rejected all ascriptions of majesty to Jesus" and suggests that "only Jesus seems capable of having been its source, or someone else who had a very accurate and equally profound grasp of Jesus' self-understanding."[2] The wilderness ordeal clearly and decisively refuses to associate Jesus with any claims to political power or social prestige. As such, it represents one of the most authentic descriptions of Jesus in the Christian scriptures. Whether it summarizes a series of lifetime enticements Jesus faces as he clarifies himself and his mission or embodies observations of his life by those who know him best, the wilderness account is a metaphorical event that conveys something true about Jesus of Nazareth: he remains steadfast in his refusal to turn to fame and control to make his life easier or his ministry popular.

The wilderness, *eremia* in Greek, is described as a desert, a place of solitude where loneliness, isolation, and hardship are one's companions. Ripe for archetypal interpretation, entering the wilderness involves treading into previously untouched areas, going into the unknown, crossing the psychic boundary between certainty and doubt, safety and risk, comfort and distress. It is a place that each of us must go, often time and time again, in order to achieve more authentic selfhood. The biblical wilderness is less a physical place than a spiritual one. Yet it is best described through concrete imagery. In the wilderness one meets wild beasts, hunger, and long days and nights devoid of companionship. Who among us has not been there?

- A twenty-year-old soldier goes to Afghanistan—his worried parents wait and pray at home.
- A young couple in a troubled marriage begins counseling.
- A woman checks into the hospital for surgery that will require months of recuperation—if it goes well.
- An elderly woman makes the difficult choice to leave her home of forty-seven years and move into assisted living.

Wilderness experiences offer clarifications to each of us similar to those extended to Jesus: What am I made of inside? How will I act when I find myself alone, abandoned, without my usual resources and comforts? What inner reserve can I call upon when temptation to escape threatens to engulf me? What vision do I hold in my heart to help me survive this situation? Lonely, unfamiliar places can strengthen my resolve and refine my choices. They can help me remember that I want to be a person of generosity and kindness, that I can endure hard things without becoming irritable and demanding. The desert can be a forbidding place, but it also hides beauty that blooms in its own time.

IN THE WILDERNESS

All of the wilderness narratives begin when Jesus, freshly emerged from the baptismal waters, "is led by the spirit" or "driven" to the *eremia*. He takes with him a profound mystical confirmation of God's love for him—a newly strengthened self-love. The differing synoptic accounts highlight a fundamental truth about the wilderness: Sometimes a spiritual force within, a holy coercion, compels us to enter it. But we have choices. Human instincts of avoidance and denial can convince us not to go there. Other times the wilderness thrusts itself upon us. We are driven there, ready or not, to face the challenge, the loss, the pain that has exploded into our lives without invitation. Either way, if we enter into it, feel its emptiness, taste its dryness, and resist the pull to fill the void as quickly as possible and leave the arid place, angels might wait on us. That is the bible's way of saying that in time (perhaps a very long time) we might emerge from the wilderness as Jesus did: filled with holy power. For both John the Baptist and Jesus, coming out of the wilderness is associated with empowerment, with greater certainty about themselves and their purpose. The same can be true for each of us. We return to face life stronger, more sure of our destiny. But once we have been there, the memory of the wilderness will be forever in us—a reminder that we have faced the night and inhaled the stars.

Jesus could have gone directly from the waters of the Jordan to the adulation of the crowds, passing up the desert. No one would have blamed him for it. But instinct told him he needed to visit this place and let it visit him. The wilderness that he encounters is inhabited by forces that attempt to pull him away from his truest self.

Often called the temptations in the desert/wilderness, the Greek word *peirazo* ("tempt") also means "examine." What was

it that Jesus needed to examine at the start of his public ministry—or alternatively, what did the early Christian community
want to emphasize about the meaning and purpose of his life?
Would he be a political messiah who would organize a revolu-
tion to overthrow the occupying Roman forces? Would he model
his ministry after prophets like Elijah, whose exuberant and violent destruction of the prophets of competing religions is leg-
endary (1 Kgs 18:40)? These are questions faced by Christians
then and now. Will we use force to convince others that we are
right and they are wrong? Will we inflict punishment on those
who don't accept our God, mocking them as did Elijah, and gloat-
ing over their demise? Will the symbols of priest, prophet, and
king influence us more than images of a suffering servant whose
only royal title was a bloody sign on his cross?

DISCOVERING THE WILDERNESS

The three temptations, or examinations, tell us something about
the vision and values that informed Jesus' relationship to God.
Through each of them, Jesus explores how he will use his power,
how he understands his mission, and what he expects of God. In
each temptation account Jesus appeals to his Jewish religious
heritage for his response—thereby identifying the source of the
convictions that helped shape the early Christian community.
Each of the trials offers a metaphorical interpretation that can
take us in many directions. What do they mean for us today?
How do they speak to the communities of modern-day Christians who claim to follow Jesus? How far into the wilderness,
into an examination of life, can we go with him?

"Command these stones to become loaves of bread." Get your
needs met by issuing commands. Fill yourself. Satisfy your immediate desires. Don't depend on God or anyone else. Let the
resources of the earth be yours and yours alone. Use them in any
way you wish, even if it means forcing them to become something that is not in their nature. Trust your life to your ability to
control and manipulate.

For someone who had just heard a voice declaring him beloved of God, the lure of special treatment and magical powers
could have been very real. Surely a God who loved him would
not want him to suffer, to have his hungers go unmet for one
more moment. He was famished. Could he not claim just a little
privilege due a son of God? How far could he push his power?

"Throw yourself down." The use of the Greek *ballo* ("throw")
suggests an attempt to manipulate God. Go ahead, do something
impulsive or dramatic. God will protect you, directly interven-
ing in your life to open doors, create opportunities, and keep you
from harm—even the harm you might cause yourself by making
bad choices. Angels are standing by just for you!

There are endless possibilities when it comes to plumbing the
meaning of metaphors. While *ballo* is usually translated "throw,"
it can also mean "put"—as in "put yourself down" or "put down
your self." Though such a usage does not suggest an airborne
departure from the pinnacle of the Temple and is not the form
the trial took in the tradition of the evangelists, it is the other
side of a temptation to test God's willingness to give special treatment to some and not others. God will do everything for you, or
conversely, God will do nothing. It shifts the emphasis on God
from an overindulgent presence to a neglectful one. The inner
voice of this temptation says you matter less than others—you
are inferior or even worthless. If God cares for you at all, you will
have to have some proof.

This form of self-negation can stem from insufficient early
affirmation, internalized societal messages, or even distorted religious beliefs. It tempts one to maintain an asceticism of unworthiness that ensures low self-esteem. Anytime I give in to the
temptation to keep a low profile, to expect little by way of goodness in life, and defer to others out of a denial of my worth, I may
be putting God to the test of saving me. The patriarchal expectation of silent obedience is self-negation in its institutionalized
form.

This particular interpretation of putting God to the test is not
synonymous with the deprivation and degradation imposed on
individuals from the outside, rendering them helpless to escape

from poverty, war, abuse, trafficking, and other forms of human subjugation. The exploited are not putting God to the test. Rather, it is the reverse—exploitation in all forms represents the collective temptation of the entitled to act as if God has favorites and does not mind if a few feet are dashed against a stone as long as their pursuit of power is protected. The privileged can control who lands in the hands of angels.

For Jesus, a jump off the pinnacle will certainly test how far God will go to save him from certain oblivion. Feeling the danger of the wilderness closing in, a fantasy of God sending angels to "bear you up" lest you "dash your foot against a stone" is appealing. It can call up images of quick fame, of easy escape from hardship, of knight-in-shining-armor rescues. But Jesus is not seduced into living an enchanted life. He will expect neither entitlements nor triumphal displays of God's partiality. He won't try to exert control over God or angels.

"Fall down and worship me." In the world of Jesus, falling down in worship meant to prostrate oneself. It was a sign accorded kings and dignitaries to affirm their superiority. The temptation is about placing allegiance in a world where many things compete for our devotion—splendid kingdoms and lavish homes, military might and corporate domination, personal wealth and celebrity distinction. It is also about our own private demands for loyalty from others. "Fall down and worship me." How many ways can any of us say that to those in our homes and places of work, in our relationships, within our closest circle of companions? Give me all your attention, time, energy. I want things my way. Don't disagree with me. If you cross me, you will be punished, given the silent treatment, excommunicated. I am the CEO. I'm in charge. A little compromise in spiritual integrity is a small price to pay for all that can be gained from the top of the mountain.

Like Jesus, we can each see a horizon of possibilities for our loyalty. Many shrines compete for my zeal. The *demon* may be a symbolic representation of malevolence, but it does embody a force of evil that is very real, pulling and tugging in every imaginable direction of selfishness. Jesus encounters every human temptation that the wilderness experience describes. He faces down many demons over the course of his life. So do you and I.

The Christian community remembers Jesus as one whose commitment is clear. Perhaps he came to that clarity in a single trip to the wilderness. Or he may have faced continuous challenges and undergone many desert experiences, as did the community that followed him. Few of us will be tempted to turn stones to bread, worship a devil, or take a dive off a church steeple with the hope that God will arrange a safe landing. But we will have to reckon with the metaphorical demons that live in our heads, trying to convince us that there is an easy way out of pain, a fast track to happiness, or a reward for giving prominence to our own personal demons.

PRIEST, PROPHET, KING

The wilderness narrative addresses the three most common expectations of Israel's Davidic king. The hoped-for anointed one would be a priest, a prophet, or a king—or embody all three roles. Each of these titles is open to interpretation. Each can ring of power, supremacy, and privilege, or of compassion, vision, and leadership. What Jesus does in the wilderness, and over the course of his life, is wrestle with the familiar distortions of what it means to be anointed of God. He will not work a miracle to turn stones into bread for himself, but he will find bread for the people who come looking for nourishment for their lives. He will not throw himself off the pinnacle of the Temple to test God's love for him, but he will climb the pinnacle of the cross in his faithful pursuit of nonviolent love. He will not worship anything that detracts from his steadfast commitment to the reign of God, but he will offer gentle compassion toward genuinely bewildered seekers.

Jesus leaves the wilderness the same way he enters it—in the companionship of the Holy Spirit. This invites us to remember that Jesus is not really alone in the wilderness, nor are the demon and the wild beasts his only companions there. While the *eremia* can symbolize all that is isolating and desolate, the Spirit of holiness that fills Jesus remains a constant presence. It is that same presence that fills our wilderness places today, even when we don't feel it.

PUT TO THE TEST

The trials that summarize what Jesus experiences during his life are an echo of the temptations faced by every human being. Sin goes by many names. But its essential characteristic is turning away from love, exchanging compassion for self-indulgent attitudes and behaviors. What Jesus does in the desert places of his life offers a response for each of us to emulate. One of the most striking examples of his reaction to temptation is his readiness to confront it when it looms before him. He knows what he believes. A vision lives within him, ready to be consulted when he most needs it.

Preparation can help any of us who face hard decisions. Hunger, from any one of my appetites, can be overpowering. Knowing when to take a risk and when to play it safe isn't always clear. I can be caught off guard when competing loyalties confront me. This is where short trips to the intentional wilderness can be helpful: A few minutes of prayer. A day set aside for reflection. A retreat. Regular scripture reading. If I clarify the vision by which I want to live and keep it in the forefront of my awareness, it can be a ready resource in the unexpected desert, or the larger wilderness. A friend of mine put it this way:

> I am an introvert in a position of management. Often people come to me wanting an immediate response to a request that I am not prepared to give. My temptation has always been to please others, so I used to respond too quickly, then regret it later. Now, I have a couple of immediate responses ready that respect both myself and others. I say, "I know you would prefer an immediate answer, but it would be helpful for me to give your idea some serious thought—OK?" Then I make sure I get back to the person within a day or so. I want to be a considerate person, but I don't want to be backed into a corner.

The biblical accounts identify different kinds of tests or trials—those that come from the inside, as described in the wilderness ordeal, and those that come from the outside. The evangelists describe occasions in which Jesus is confronted not by his
own interior struggles but by people who wished to snare him:

> *The Pharisees came and began to argue with him,*
> *asking for a sign from heaven, to test him. (Mk 8:11)*

> *Then the Pharisees went and plotted to entrap him*
> *in what he said.*
> *But Jesus, aware of their malice, said,*
> *"Why are you putting me to the test,*
> *you hypocrites?" (Mt 22:15, 18)*

The queries of the Pharisees were not authentic—they were co-
vert attempts to trick Jesus, to set him up for political suicide, to
expose him to ridicule, to diminish his influence.

Several years ago the late Father Raymond Brown was the
featured speaker at a Midwestern symposium on scripture. He
had recently been criticized by biblical literalists for his commentary on the immaculate conception of Mary, and his presence at the symposium had been controversial. When he finished his presentation and began a discussion with the audience,
a woman seated in the front row emphatically raised her hand:
"Father Brown," she said pointedly, "do you believe in the immaculate conception?" Raymond Brown recognized the trick
question for what it was—an attempt to force him into an abrupt
public challenge of church teaching. He took off his glasses, leaned
slowly forward on the podium, and looked at the woman.
"Madam," he said with great courtesy, "I believe that every conception is immaculate. May I have the next question?" The audience of several hundred people clapped and cheered. The woman
who had posed the question scowled. Her hidden agenda had
been both exposed and foiled by someone who was prepared to
be clever as a serpent and innocent as a dove.

We live in times not unlike those of Jesus. Turning words into
weapons and using questions as traps, any one of us can attempt

to discredit others, embarrass them, or even distort what they have said to shore up our opposing positions. We see this in political circles, religious forums, and everyday encounters in the workplace, neighborhood, and home. Even the evening news can become a partisan hotbed of verbal slaughter as newscasters depart from reporting the news to disparaging those who do not support their particular agenda. Family members assault one another with a barrage of questions aimed less at gaining information and more at insulting or duping someone they are supposed to love. Using letters to the editor to vilify someone whose view I oppose, tape recording homilies to find evidence of dissent, combing the writings of theologians to find something to report to Rome—all are indications that behavior in the Christian community has sunk to a new low, all in the name of God. In the war for control, dominance, and resources, the trials that Jesus faced in the wilderness find expression in every age.

Anytime I look for ways to catch another in a mistake, overpower a companion in a conversation, or back someone into a corner, I am standing in opposition to the reign of God. I have sacrificed compassion for control, exchanged truth for deception—both of which have a demonic tone. Evil lurks in the wilderness of trickery. Jesus might have been *led* to the wilderness, or even *driven* there by the Spirit, but it was not the Spirit of God that tempted him. Deliberately putting others to the test is not spirit-led behavior. The wilderness accounts are a reminder that it is not our job to put others on trial.

DO NOT BRING US TO THE TIME OF TRIAL

When the disciples ask Jesus to teach them how to pray, he offers them a simple prayer. Reproduced in two different versions, in Matthew and in Luke, most scholars believe that the Lucan formulation is closest to the earliest source.[3] However, each version helps us understand what was important to the community that prayed it.

At the end of the prayer in the Lucan version is this petition: "Do not bring us to the time of trial" (Lk 11:4). Matthew adds, "but rescue us from the evil one" (Mt 6:13). Understanding the meaning of this final petition in the prayer that Jesus taught his disciples requires a closer look at its history, since it has come to us through many evolutions both in language and interpretation. Matthew inherited the prayer in Aramaic, the language Jesus spoke, and translated it into crude Greek in the second century. Matthew's version was used to translate the entire prayer into Latin. By the seventeenth century the King James Bible had produced a translation from the Latin into English by way of Old English. Since original meaning can easily be lost in multiple translations, many scholars today look to the early Aramaic version of the prayer to gain new insights. How are we to understand the words: "And do not bring us to the test" (often translated, "lead us not into temptation")?

Aramaic is a poetic language that invites us to feel the rhythm of each word, intuiting its message. Every line of the Lord's Prayer, indeed every word, can be translated in different ways. Looking at the final petition, the following translation from the Aramaic is close to the original sense of the prayer:

> *Wela tachlân l'nesjuna:* Let us not be lost in superficial things (materialism, common temptations).
> *ela patzân min bischa:* but let us be freed
> from that which keeps us off from our true purpose.[4]

"Let us not be lost in superficial things": Help us not get confused about what is most important. Keep us from shallow thinking and insincere actions. Don't allow us to give in to impulsive desires. Walk with us in the desert places of life.

"Let us be freed from that which keeps us off from our true purpose": Keep us on the path of discipleship. Help us know ourselves well and to stay focused on love and justice. Untie us from anxiety and free us from worry. Release us from negative thinking and critical judgments of our brothers and sisters.

The vision in the final petition of the prayer that Jesus taught reflects his mission. As he moves about Judea, finding the lost and freeing the captives from any number of ailments is a way of life for him. The early Christian community remembers him not only *teaching* these words, but *living* them. For the woman of John's gospel "caught in adultery" (Jn 8:3), release from those who want to stone her sends a strong signal about patriarchal oppression that entraps women while allowing men to go free. The nameless woman who is delivered from evil that day is a model for all women seeking freedom from the trial of inequality. Her bent-over sister who is "quite unable to stand up straight" (Lk 13:11) faces crippling burdens of a different kind. She too finds liberation from whatever it is that weighs her down when she meets the man who does not wish captivity for anyone. The frightened father whose son has a spirit that makes him unable to speak, dashing him down when it seizes him (Mk 9:17–18), the blind man of Bethsaida (Mk 8:22), the paralyzed man (Lk 5:18), and countless others held hostage by trials of infirmity that test their patience and drain their spirit meet the Jesus who makes good on the prayer of his heart: Do not bring us to the time of trial. Rescue us from all manner of evil. Don't let them be lost. Free them to follow their true purpose. If we pray this prayer, we also ask to live it.

PETITIONING GOD

Abwoon d'bwashmaya
Nethqadash shmakh
Teytey malkuthakh
Nehwey tzevyanach aykanna d'bwashmaya aph b'arha.
Hawvlan lachma d'sunqanan yaomana.
Washboqlan khaubayn (wakhtahayn)
aykana daph khnan shbwoqan l'klayyabayn.
Wela tahlan l'nesyuna
Ela patzan min bisha.
Metol dilakhie malkutha wahaya wateshbukhta l'ahlam almin.
Ameyn.[5]

"Oh, Mama," they said softly, as they sat on the floor in the customary position for prayer in their culture. "You are within and around us." The words of the young nuns in Bangladesh rang truer to the original Aramaic that Jesus prayed with his disciples than any I had ever heard. Whenever they prayed together in the tongue that was most familiar to them, I could hear ancient Semitic sounds in their native language.

Requests voiced in the Lord's Prayer, or the prayer to the Mama, as it can also be translated, are unadorned hopes for the simplest things: that God's way of unity will come into all hearts, that God's desire and ours will be the same, that everyone will have bread and wisdom, that the cords of our mistakes will be released, that we will untie the bonds of those who have offended us, that surface things will not delude us, and that we will be freed from all that holds us back from true freedom.

Prayer of petition is a familiar form of prayer among all of us who turn to God with the deepest longing of our hearts. The petitions that Jesus suggests to his disciples are unpretentious pleas for food and forgiveness, for God's way to become our way. Prayers of petition are part of the eucharistic liturgy in which, as a community, we ask for peace, for safety, for healing, and for support in the wilderness.

But sometimes the prayer of petition is reduced to requests for superficial things: good weather for a picnic, unmerited success, winning the lottery, even scoring touchdowns and finding parking places. A recent television program showed a bride and her mother in the foyer of an upscale bridal salon saying a quick prayer that she would find the perfect wedding dress—a petition that could make even God discouraged. There is nothing wrong with having a conversation with God about our immediate needs or most pressing desires. But novenas to alter global weather patterns so I have sunshine for my vacation is probably not what Jesus had in mind in teaching his disciples how to pray. Nor is the final petition of the most famous prayer for Christians concerned with deliverance from a devil named Satan. Rather, it is an ardent desire to be freed from anything that keeps us from becoming more fully human, more ready to incarnate the holy.

THE SYMBOLISM OF THE ADVERSARY

The force of evil is variously translated in the Christian writings. In the ordeal in the wilderness, the figurative devil (*diabolos* in Greek, meaning "slanderer") is the main player, although Satan (*satanas*, meaning "adversary") is identified as the tempter in Mark's gospel. The use of the Greek *demon* (*daimon*, meaning "evil spirit") in the Christian writings commonly describes those believed to be possessed—a prescientific attempt to attribute the causes of mental illness to demonic forces taking possession of a person. Made popular by the film *The Exorcist*, demonic possession is just that—a movie—an attempt to tell a story about evil. *The Exorcist* was one of a series of horror films called demonic child movies, along with *Rosemary's Baby* and *The Omen*, produced in the 1960s and 1970s. Their popularity is attributed, in part, to a public need to externalize evil, to have it out in the open where it can be seen and in some measure controlled. A rash of suspected demonic possessions and requests for exorcisms followed the release of these films—offering more support for scientific studies about human suggestibility than demonic possession.

In addition to Hollywood creations much popular understanding about the figure of Satan is owed not to the bible but to Milton's *Paradise Lost*, a seventeenth-century epic wherein the rebellious Satan is hurled out of heaven to earth. While Milton's Satan and the biblical symbols of evil are not synonymous, graphic depictions of a fallen angel named Satan have contributed to the personification of evil in religious sentiment.

The Greek words used in scripture to describe evil impulses and antagonism to goodness are symbolic—figurative images that seek to make the message more real. Even though these words in the Christian stories have sometimes been personified—given an actual personal existence—they remain anthropomorphic representations of the presence of evil. It has been tempting to assign blame for all the malevolence in the world to a bad angel named

Satan who sneaks around in the shadows looking for souls to ensnare. It releases human beings from taking full responsibility for whatever evil their actions entail.

Resisting belief in a personified devil is in no way a denial of the presence of sin and evil in the world. Nor does it oppose recognition of the many forces within and without that tempt human beings to be self-serving, cruel, and dishonest. Maybe it is easier to believe that the sources of wrongdoing live outside of me, that impulses to lie, cheat, steal, and kill are not really part of who I am but rather have their *real* source in a devil—a person with a different name from mine. Then, the sinful temptations I have to resist are outside of me instead of within me. Such a belief leaves me fundamentally innocent, always able to say, "The devil made me do it!"

THE MANY FACES OF TEMPTATION

The words of the disciples caught in a windstorm that swamped their boat are familiar: "Lord, save us! We are perishing!" (Mt 8:25). Matthew is writing for the early church in its fragile and threatened state. That cry to be saved from extinction describes their circumstances more than once as the fledgling community of believers faces a variety of storms. One temptation is to fear that a storm will be their undoing, that rough experiences will so shake their convictions that the Christian community will not survive. A second is to doubt Jesus, to have diminished faith in who he is and in who he is showing them to become. Walter Wink has an interesting interpretation about the storm at sea, based on the disciples' question once the sea had calmed down: "What sort of man is this, that even the winds and the sea obey him?" (Mt 8:27). "What the disciples wondered was not what kind of divine being Jesus was, but what sort of human being is this?"[6] For Wink, this is a critical question because the disciples are learning how to incarnate the same God who is being made incarnate in Jesus. A third temptation is to settle too quickly for divinity to explain Jesus, and abandon the journey—to excuse ourselves from the same task of becoming the incarnate of God, fully human individuals who look to Jesus less as a savior and more as a model for our own voyage into the human condition. If divinity identifies Jesus more than humanity, the standard for our own growth in holiness is set much higher—too high to reach and impossible to attain fully. It is a great excuse!

The storm at sea is a metaphor for a number of trials faced by the early church and by each one of us in our lives. While the trials we face today might be different, the experience of feeling apprehensive, trapped in pain, or enslaved by temptation is as familiar to us as it was to the people of the first century who sought Jesus out to free them from whatever held them bound.

The gospel narratives that tell of healings and miraculous release are meant to invite us to internalize the way of Jesus so that we too can invite burdened people to stand up straight, to come closer, to be isolated no longer. No less than Jesus, you and I are called to create conditions in the human community that bring about true equality, where blindness gives way to light, enslavement to freedom, and paralysis to the dance of justice.

PRAY THAT YOU MAY NOT COME
INTO THE TIME OF TRIAL

In Gethsemane Jesus again brings up the issue of temptation with his disciples: "Pray that you may not come into the time of trial" (Mk 14:38). It is a reprise of the prayer he gave them earlier. It is the elemental prayer of petition—expressed in a Greek word (*erchomai*) that has several possible translations. Pray that you do not "enter into" temptation, pray that you do not follow it, stay with it, become part of it, or return to it. Jesus assumes that trials will come to the disciples, but he warns them not to get inside of the "time of trial," or not to let it get inside of them. Theologically, the time of trial to which Jesus refers is the symbolic eschatological trial that is directed toward the end times. But what does that mean? Disciples, whether in Jesus' time or in the early church or today, face the same trial that confronts Jesus in the wilderness: Turn these stones into bread. Fall down and worship me. Jump off the pinnacle of the Temple. It is the temptation to disregard the invitation of the reign of God. It is the temptation to forget all the hungry people, to ignore justice, to doubt that God's way is possible.

The Greek-English New Testament has a compelling translation of the word *peirasmos* ("temptation" or "trial"), rendering it "pressure."[7] This same translation is used in all the synoptic narratives of the wilderness ordeal where Jesus is "pressured" by the slanderer. The word suggests weight, a force that does not let up. While not a usual translation, it offers another way of imaging the trials that any of us might experience. Often, there is a sense of strain that no amount of resisting can overcome. Temptation pushes against us, creating a pressure that can be debilitating. It wears us down over time.

Words slant things. Trials, temptations, ordeals, and pressures mean different things to different people. But however the word *temptation* is understood, it involves the urge to turn away from the holy when it seems to ask too much. Whether the lure is strong or faint, of greater or lesser consequence, a biblical trial is an enticement to turn away from our true purpose. To meet a trial in the wilderness is to come upon it when we are the most defenseless, when resources to resist are weak.

Jesus repeatedly advises the disciples then and now how to live, how to pray, how to face temptation. Keep your eyes focused on the holy. "Not my will but yours be done" (Lk 22:42). Perhaps Jesus was talking as much to himself as to his disciples as the din of those who were coming to arrest him grew louder.

We can only speculate today as to what those words might have meant—whether Jesus actually uttered them, or whether they were formulated for him by the early church to convey the depth of his trust in the midst of suffering. "Not my will but yours"—the words sound unreservedly human. He knows his message has repeatedly alienated the political and religious authorities. He is praying in a garden as the angry mob makes its way toward him. At what point would he have heard their voices? "Not my will." What might someone in his situation have willed?

That those who were so enraged could understand the way of peace? That the suffering he anticipated could be reduced or even eliminated? That he could have more time? What do any of us wish for in the midst of anguish that claims our dreams?

Chapter 7

Transfiguration

Being Transformed along the Way

Six days later, Jesus took with him Peter and James and John,
and led them up a high mountain apart, by themselves.
And he was transfigured before them,
and his clothes became dazzling white,
such as no one on earth could bleach them.
And there appeared to them Elijah with Moses,
who were talking with Jesus.
Then Peter said to Jesus, "Rabbi, it is good for us to be here;
let us make three dwellings,
one for you, one for Moses, and one for Elijah."
He did not know what to say, for they were terrified.
Then a cloud overshadowed them,
and from the cloud there came a voice,
"This is my Son, the Beloved; listen to him!"
Suddenly when they looked around,
they saw no one with them any more,
but only Jesus. (Mk 9:2–8)

Now about eight days after these sayings, Jesus took with him
Peter, John and James, and went up on the mountain to pray.
And while he was praying, the appearance of his face changed,
and his clothes became dazzling white.
Suddenly they saw two men, Moses and Elijah, talking to him.

They appeared in glory and were speaking of his departure,
Which he was about to accomplish at Jerusalem.
Now Peter and his companions were weighed down with sleep;
but since they had stayed awake,
they saw his glory and the two men
who stood with him. (Lk 9:28–32)

He changed over the course of their knowing him. He became more luminous, more transparent. There were times when the disciples didn't quite know how to understand it, much less describe it to others. But here, in the two transfiguration accounts, the evangelists tried to interpret the tradition they had inherited, a tradition that carried the early church's conviction that Jesus was the son of God. They had experienced such overwhelming certainty of this over time that a story would help convey the truth of it. "Thus the story is seen as the externalization of an inner spiritual event—whether pre- or post-Easter is impossible to say."[1] Metaphors, unbound by time, can reveal their truth without the constraint of dates. Whether before or after Easter, six days as Mark asserts or eight as Luke reports, is immaterial to the integrity of a great spiritual insight that is not dependent on a calendar for its veracity.

Have you ever known someone whose transformation so astonished you that you could hardly believe what you were seeing? Has someone close to you become gentler, wiser, or more self-aware? Did he soften his ragged edges? Did she gladden her spirit? We are accustomed to people changing slowly, mellowing over time. What the disciples of Jesus experienced may have been similar—a transformation that suddenly got their attention!

Transfiguration (metamorphoo in Greek) is an oblique word. Most simply, it describes "change" or "an alteration in form." While familiar in the Mediterranean world, it is rare in the gospels, and even Luke does not use the word in his transfiguration account. Most likely, he did not wish to confuse his readers by introducing a theme that could associate Jesus with the magical changes of form often seen in pagan heroes of antiquity. "This motif of metamorphoses is so common in classical paganism (cf. Ovid, *Metamorphoses*) that Luke judged it best to avoid the term altogether."[2] In sensitivity to his predominantly Gentile audience, Luke wants to ensure that the mystery the disciples experience on the mountain is not misinterpreted as a spectacle arranged by pagan gods but a genuine manifestation of the holy God. But for Matthew and Mark, Jesus is *transfigured*—they see him in a new way and can only interpret it as a revelation of his truest identity.

THE GOD WHO SPEAKS ON MOUNTAINS

In the Hebrew bible events that occur on mountains are symbolic of revelation; God speaks on mountains. For ancient peoples the highest places in the land were closest to the heavens, the supposed dwelling place of the gods, a notion adopted by the Hebrews (Is 14:13; Ps 48:3). One of the early references for God in the Pentateuch is El Shaddai—commonly understood as "the One of the Mountain."[3] The Akkadian word for mountain, *shadu*, may have been an early root of the word. Though the exact translation of *El Shaddai* is uncertain, the designation *El* is a common reference for any god in the Semitic world.[4] While it is impossible to know the earliest source of the many designations of Israel's God, "it seems almost certain that the God of the Jews evolved gradually from the Canaanite El, who was in all likelihood the 'God of Abraham.'"[5]

Since ancient peoples worshiped their deities in shrines located in high places, there is an historical precedent for viewing El Shaddai as the God (or One) of the mountain. However, early translations into Greek might have understood *shaddai* as having its source in the Hebrew *shadad*, meaning "overpower," supporting the translation of *El Shaddai* as "Almighty God"—the rendering in the NRSV, for example. But there have been challenges to this as an exclusive interpretation. The Hebrew *shad (shadaim)* means "breast." Does the name El Shaddai carry a hint of an earlier understanding of a maternal nourishing deity—a breasted One? Those who argue that *shad* is a proper derivation for El Shaddai note that the name was originally connected to a deity specifically tied to birth and fertility.[6] Though the designation in the Hebrew bible concerns a male deity, it remains possible that the understanding of El Shaddai transitioned as monotheism, with its male God, first absorbed and then obscured earlier meanings.

Early peoples commonly looked to their surroundings to inform their understanding of life. Nature gave them ample visual cues. The languages of indigenous people are replete with words that reflect their physical world. If a deity is believed to be like a caring mother who feeds and looks after her children, an ample, rounded mountain offers an image of a breasted one. When a god is thought to be a male deity who dwells in high places, a mountain again furnishes an apt metaphor. Often words and names given by native populations are changed by those who come later. Popular lore has it that the Chinook Nation of the Pacific Northwest was the source of the original name, Tahoma ("large breast"), of the majestic mountain in western Washington now called Mount Rainier. Claimed to come from *ta-toosh*—Chinook jargon for "breast" or "milk"—the word described a mountain that bore an obvious visual resemblance to a large rounded breast.

In the Hebrew bible mountains are associated with the most important communications between God and the leaders of the people. On these high places human insights into the nature of the holy often take place. It is on an unnamed mountain, in a narrative that may represent a major turning point in ending child sacrifice, that Abraham is stopped from killing his son Isaac in customary offering of the firstborn son (Gn 22:12). Moses encounters a God of tender seeking in the burning bush on Mount Horeb (also called Sinai) and learns that the place is "holy ground" (Ex 3:1–2). It is here that God reveals the divine name YHWH (Yahweh) (Ex 3:14–15). This name—impossible to define fully—will become the most common reference for the incomprehensible God of the Hebrew bible. In a gradually unfolding theophany Moses receives the commandments and the tablets of the covenant on Mount Sinai (Ex 19:20; 31:18). On the mountain Moses enters the cloud that signifies God's presence, spending a symbolic forty days and nights communing with the holy one (Ex 24:18). In evocative imagery Moses literally *walks into God* in the vivid narrative where a devouring fire announces God's presence and a portentous cloud invites penetration. Later, on Mount Nebo, Moses is shown all of the land that will be given to his descendants (Dt 34:1). On the same mountain Moses has his last communication with God before his death.

Elijah meets this same God, now called the Lord, on the mountain Horeb, though the outward manifestation of the presence of the holy one has changed. Gone for now are the accompanying smoke and fire, and dramatic displays of power. Here, God passes by in "a sound of sheer silence" (1 Kgs 19:12). No longer crashing into the people's consciousness with earthquakes and rock-smashing winds that command their attention, God now moves about the mountain in absolute stillness. Elijah, with his face covered, leans out of the darkness of the cave where he is hiding to hear the voice of the Lord. The question put to him is eschatological: "What are you doing here, Elijah?" It is a question any one of us might hear at different times in our lives. How did you get to this place in your human journey? What path have you followed? Why are you *here*—hiding, running, covered up? Elijah's response is starkly familiar—he tells God what everyone else has done that caused him to end up in this place of isolation and terror. God listens, then tells Elijah to continue on his way. The same message might be given to us when our life journey comes to a halt, when we don't know which way to turn. For Elijah, continuing on his way took him to the wilderness, a possible destination for us as well.

For Abraham, Moses, and Elijah, interactions with God on the mountain bear all the noise and drama of an Oscar-worthy cinematographic thriller. At times the content of God's directives bears the primitive tone of the culture. As the people's understanding of true holiness develops, God's word shines with profundity: Do not hurt a child (Gn 22:12). You are standing on holy ground (Ex 3:5). I hear and see and feel the suffering of my people, and so must you (Ex 3:7–8). Honor one another. Tell the truth. Be faithful. Take care of those who are without resources. Welcome those you consider "other" (Ex 20:12–17; 22:21–25). The content of the mountain messages will deepen over time as the people continue to meet the God who nourishes, who cares for them like a mother, who stays with them always. As time goes on the figure of God is gradually *transfigured*, becoming less angry, less prone to punish the people for their failings. The God that Jesus encounters on the mountain has no more wrath—only words of loving encouragement. Reminiscent of the affirmation Jesus experienced at this baptism, the God of his ancestors speaks of love and listening—to him and to us.

The commonalities among the gods of the ancients and that of the Hebrews have both fascinated and puzzled biblical scholars. The term *transfiguration* may apply as much to the constantly shifting notions of the deity as it does to whatever it was that the early Christian community associated with a transformation of Jesus. Was Jesus transfigured, or was the way he was perceived transformed? Or, was it a little of both—Jesus changed over time and so did his disciples' understanding of him? Placing the event on a mountain may have as much significance as the event itself. It helps ensure that future readers will understand that God is present in the transfiguration mystery.

As you reflect on your own spiritual journey, how has your understanding of God changed? Do you see transition between your earliest notion of God and how you view the holy one today? How would you have described God five, twenty, or fifty years ago? If your perception of God has been transformed, you have entered into the mystery of transfiguration. Like the awe-struck disciples on the mountain, you have been inside the cloud where God and humans talk.

The actual mountain where the transfiguration of Jesus occurs is disputed, although Mount Tabor has been celebrated as its site since the fourth century. Trying to isolate a particular mountain where the event took place might enrich its believability, but it also externalizes and therefore diminishes its mystical quality. Since the transfiguration experience is an inner, spiritual one, its true location is in the heart. Released from physical geography, it transcends time and space. The ground on which we stand is always holy, and every mountain in the world is a worthy place to meet the living God.

It was not only the people of antiquity who gazed at mountain peaks and felt the enormity and majesty of something beyond themselves. The sound of sheer silence can be heard today on Alaska's Mount Denali. Successfully scaling Mount Everest leaves the climber transformed forever. Clouds often overshadow Mount Rainier, and from within them is the same voice that Jesus and the disciples heard: Love is present. Listen.

ALONE AND AT PRAYER

If mountains are associated with biblical experiences of the holy, being at prayer is another. Particularly for Luke, who alone reports that Jesus and his disciples went up the mountain "to pray," significant transformation and prayer are often intertwined. Luke portrays Jesus at prayer more than the other three gospels combined. Though he took part in regular synagogue worship and was familiar with the spiritual writings of his people (Lk 4:16, 17), the image of Jesus alone at prayer is prominent. It is while at prayer, after his baptism in Luke's gospel, that Jesus has an overwhelming experience of God's love (Lk 3:21–22). Following an intense night with the hurting crowds, he departed at daybreak "and went to a deserted place" (Lk 4:42). As word spread about his ability to inspire and heal, and the crowds gathered, "he would withdraw to deserted places and pray" (Lk 5:16). In preparation to select the Twelve, "he spent the night in prayer to God" (Lk 6:12).

Jesus seems able to live his life in the context of intimate communication with God, moving between formal prayer and human conversation with ease:

Once when Jesus was praying alone, with only the disciples near him,
he asked them, "Who do the crowds say that I am?"
They answered, "John the Baptist; but others, Elijah;
and still others, that one of the ancient prophets has arisen."
He said to them, "But who do you say that I am?"
Peter answered, "The Messiah of God." (Lk 9:18–20)

These are the sort of questions that come to one in prayer: Who am I, really? How are others experiencing me? What effect does my presence have on those who encounter me? How well do those I care most about really know me? While Luke is providing his readers with a pivotal theological statement about Jesus' identity, he is also, perhaps unintentionally, offering a portrait of a prayerful spirit. Prayer isn't separate from life. It doesn't take us away from our relational concerns but rather more deeply into them. A person of genuine prayer moves between many levels of holy attentiveness, often simultaneously. Like the ebb and flow of the tides, prayerfulness is a rhythmic dance back and forth, in and out of a presence that is beyond containment, at once here and now and utterly beyond categories of human confinement. There are times when my prayer disquiets me with challenges I would rather not hear. Other times prayer is as comforting as the softness of the light on an ocean wave just before it crests. Some forms of prayer transport us into that wordless place of mystical union where time stands still. Other spiritual experiences, like births and sunrises, offer moments of ecstatic awe that live on, long after the newborn sleeps and darkness has swallowed the sky.

When Jesus begins a dialogue with his disciples, he hasn't stopped praying. He has simply moved the focus of his constant familiarity with the holy to another realm. He doesn't leave God to interact with his friends. When he teaches and heals, he is also at prayer. Secure in his relationship with God, Jesus is now recognized more deeply by Peter. This context of acute mutual knowing is the usual setting for a transfiguration event—then and now, experiences of intimacy transform us.

THE APPEARANCE OF HIS FACE CHANGED

What actually happens? Is the transfiguration a single event or a gradual progression in the disciples' depth of comprehension of Jesus? Mark is the first evangelist to write about the transfiguration, and he did so with uncharacteristic elaboration. Using Mark as their model, Matthew and Luke consider the event significant enough to include in their gospels, with their distinctive modifications.

It is always difficult to describe a transformative happening to those who have not witnessed it. Words alone are inadequate. We tend to do what the evangelists did—surround the event in a descriptive narrative, appeal to the familiar, embellish the details, use color and sound to evoke the senses: Clothes that become "dazzling white" as no bleach could make them, a face shines "like the sun," long-deceased prophets talk as if alive, the familiar overshadowing cloud with a voice within. All of these are symbolic attempts to articulate the unshakable conviction that the disciples come to over time—that Jesus is held so closely in God's glory that he is part of it. They see it. He is, as Peter had confessed the week before, "the Messiah of God." A story fleshes out what they come to know in their hearts.

People's faces change. More than the physical changes associated with age or illness, a person's countenance can become altered by the circumstances of life. Sorrow has a face. Joy has a face. Every deeply internalized stance of the heart has its own manifestation. What is inside of us is mirrored in our eyes and shown in our expression. A face that "shone like the sun" is radiant. It has communed with the sages of history. It has heard an inner voice of overwhelming affirmation. It has met love.

The transfiguration account offers multiple interpretive possibilities. At first glace, it is about Jesus, who grew in wisdom and grace over time as he became ever more convinced of his mission and certain that he was truly beloved of God. It refers to the disciples and those around Jesus whose learning is transformed as they accompany the one who heals those sick of body and weary of spirit, who teaches the crowds and gives them hope, who talks with prophets and spends long nights conversing with God.

It is also about the transfiguration of the holy God, or rather, how human beings describe the holy one. God slowly loses the superficial accoutrements transferred from the gods of antiquity. Throughout the bible the perception of God is gradually transfigured from punitive judge to forgiving friend, from remote superior to compassionate companion, from a divinity who has favorites to an inclusive host who sets a table big enough for all. As the understanding of God is transformed, the aura of a stern biblical judge, reigning from a mountaintop accessible only to a few, slowly gives way to a portrait of a holy one who weeps at the death of a friend, who circulates without judgment among those whom others disdain, and who enjoys eating and drinking with anyone who shows up.

It is not that God becomes lax about rules or soft on sin. Rather, the notion of sin is transfigured along with the notion of what it means to be God. Human beings fail not when they eat corn on the Sabbath but when they ignore those who have no grain. It is not touching a corpse that contaminates them, but failing to act when the dead bodies mount up from war, starvation, and violence. As we travel more fully into the transfiguring cloud, we come to know that the commandments of Sinai can be carried by the single great commandment—the law of love. The author of this law will be provoked to wrath only when the people act without justice.

HE SET HIS FACE

The next time we hear about the face of Jesus, it is not bathed in sunlight. The glorious moment of the transfiguration event has ended, as exhilarating experiences inevitably do. We must smile in quiet recognition at Peter's impulsive suggestion to "make three dwellings" (Lk 9:33), to memorialize the experience with permanence. How great is the yearning in any of us to make special times last? I can hear myself begging my friends to stay just a little longer. When the clock strikes twelve, I wonder, with Cinderella at the end of the ball, where the time went. The bottom of the mountain calls.

Jesus and his disciples do, in fact, "come down from the mountain" (Lk 9:37). They have to. None of us, not even God's beloved, is exempt from the passage of time or the limits set by boundaries. Celebrations are like songs that come with endings. They touch our hearts and help our spirits soar—and then they are over. The rapturous emotional highs of our lives are not meant to encase us in a bubble of unending jubilation. The orgasmic pleasure of human lovemaking is time conditioned. All lovely moments give us energy for the rest of the journey, hope for our faltering spirits, anticipation that joy will visit us again.

It is after the transfiguration event that Jesus' journey assumes a somber tone: "He set his face toward Jerusalem" (Lk 9:51). In a biblical section reported by Luke alone, the journey theme picks up its pace. There are more disciples to call, more implications of God's reign to emphasize, and more people to include. And so we meet the Seventy-two, we learn that those we thought were outsiders can teach us how to be neighbors, and we are forced to acknowledge that the way of God leads to Jerusalem, where there is no escape from the cross. Like Jesus, and the early Christians, we too will have to set our faces toward the place where the costly price of discipleship is revealed.

To set my face implies an unwavering determination to go forward, to do what must be done despite obstacles, fears, or wishes that the cup that holds the agony of the task ahead can pass me by. When Jesus set his face toward Jerusalem, his resolve to honor his journey, to embrace the implications of the reign of God he had preached, was undertaken with a sense of urgency that allowed no turning back. Perhaps the transfiguration experience—as for the disciples and the early church—offers Jesus himself the mountain's strength and one more message of love from the voice that broadcasts from clouds.

BEING CHANGED

Like Jesus and the disciples, and following in the footsteps of the first Christians, the transfiguration experience beckons every disciple. Revealed less in a moment than over a lifetime, transformation is not an option for those who take the way of God seriously. When Paul writes to the Romans—even though they are a community he did not found and did not know well—he begins his advice to them about Christian living with these words:

> *Do not be conformed to this world, but be transformed*
> [metamorphoo]
> *by the renewing of your minds,*

so that you might discern what is the will of God—
what is good and acceptable and perfect. (Rom 12:1–2)

The word *metamorphoo* is the same word that will be used later
to describe the transfiguration experience of Jesus when the gospels are written. But here the word does not call up theophanous
images on mountaintops, but rather a quiet inner movement of
the heart toward goodness. For Paul, this kind of metamorphosis
is not manifested in dramatic mystical events or heady intellec-
tual beliefs, but by a change in understanding, by a renewal in
the attitude with which we approach life as Christians. He goes
on to encourage the Christians at Rome to be humble and loving. This is what constitutes being transformed. It is what transfiguration ultimately means. The same message is found in the
second letter to the Christians at Corinth:

And all of us, with unveiled faces,
seeing the glory of the Lord as though reflected in a mirror,
are being transformed [metamorphoo] *into the same image*
from one degree of glory to another;
for this comes from the Lord, the Spirit. (2 Cor 3:18)

Once again the transfiguration theme is applied to the life of
every Christian, whose privilege of seeing the same glory that
Jesus saw carries with it the transformative power of love. The
words are strong: All of us are being transformed. We are being
changed, deepened, strengthened. The holy ground of the mountain is always under our feet, and the cloud that overshadowed
Jesus and the disciples covers us as well. And if we listen carefully, a voice will always be there to tell us we are loved.

TRANSFIGURATION AS INCREASING

The Lucan nativity narrative ends with these unpretentious words:
"And Jesus increased in wisdom and in years, and in divine and
human favor" (Lk 2:52). The Greek *phronesis* ("wisdom") implies
practical wisdom, the kind of insight that one accrues through

life experience. In Luke's mind Jesus was not born with super-natural knowledge embedded in his brain. He had to learn, to make connections, to develop awareness—and no doubt, to make mistakes in the process as all learners do. We have often so "over-divinized" Jesus of Nazareth that it can be hard to imagine him as a toddler, uttering barely intelligible syllables, crying when he is hungry, and chasing birds once he learns to walk. It makes sense to think of him as a precocious child, given the incredible spiritual leap he realizes as a young adult. But we don't know. There is no *historical* record of Jesus as a baby, a child, or an adolescent.

What we do know is that he grows, he develops, and he deepens as he ages. He had to process the circumstances of his life, to learn the trade of a carpenter, and to think long and deeply about things of consequence. He studies the faith of his ancestors and learns the sayings of the prophets. The political and cultural landscape that surrounds him shapes his unusual attunement to issues of justice. This is simply to say that Jesus, like any of us, was affected by his environment.

But in addition to age-related progression in skills and cognition, there are times when new awareness intensifies in him, reaching a depth of certainty that graces him in a remarkable way. More soaring than typical "ah-ha" moments, grasps of wisdom penetrated his humanity, taking him to places that few go. Something increased in him.

There are actually many transfiguration events in the life of Jesus that are significant. The first is his baptism. Another occurs when Jesus comes out of the wilderness and goes home to Nazareth. Luke notes that it was customary for him to go to the synagogue on the Sabbath (Lk 4:16). We are told that Jesus was given the scroll of the prophet Isaiah and unrolled it. Jesus is presented as confident in what he is called to proclaim:

> *The Spirit of the Lord is upon me,*
> *because he has anointed me to bring good news to the poor.*
> *He has sent me to proclaim release to the captives*
> *and recovery of sight to the blind,*
> *to let the oppressed go free,*
> *to proclaim the year of the Lord's favor. (Lk 4:18–19)*

But something quite unusual happens that day—so atypical that those who know him hardly recognize him. He is different; something has changed in him. "All spoke well of him and were amazed at the gracious words that came from his mouth" (Lk 4:22). Jesus is in his hometown, the place where he grew up, and Luke tells us that the people in the synagogue know he is "Joseph's son" but can hardly believe it (Lk 4:22). There has been such a transformation in the way he presents himself that the people can only interpret it as *charis* ("favor"). Jesus is graced in a new way. It is visible in his demeanor as he confidently proclaims the reading and boldly applies Isaiah's message to himself. In a stunning announcement Jesus confirms what the people were seeing: "Today this scripture has been fulfilled in your hearing" (Lk 4:21). It sums up a revolutionized self-understanding, solidified both at his baptism and in whatever constitutes the wilderness experience. It represents a giant dive into the murky waters of self-understanding and a thrust toward human depth that are puzzling to those who have known him all his life.

Then, another shocking thing happens. A freshly self-proclaimed anointed one who has awed the crowd continues talking. Those who are initially inspired by his words become enraged. Jesus is preaching a God who extends outreach to *everyone*, especially the poor! How can he say such offensive things! Who does he think he is! For those who want special treatment from God, all the talk about good news for the poor and freedom for the oppressed is not good news and freedom for them. Luke's Jesus is confronting those who remain locked into an understanding of God who favors some while excluding others. This will be a theme in his preaching and teaching for the remainder of his brief ministry. It will infuriate both the civil and religious leaders. It will get him killed.[7]

Today this scripture has been fulfilled—the emphasis cannot be ignored. *Today* means every day that the message is heard. *Today* was that day in Nazareth in the synagogue. *Today* included the first-century Christian community for whom Luke is writing. *Today* is a mandate for our own times—*today*, in this time and in this place, the spirit of the holy is upon us. We have all been anointed, sent to bring good news to the poor. By our transformed actions in the world those who are held captive by anything that degrades the human spirit must be released. We are all to become less blinded by self-interest and to see our obligations to one another more clearly. Those who are burdened with debt they cannot possibly repay, whether financial or interpersonal, must be freed. The ancient forgiveness energy of the Jubilee Year is to be proclaimed once again. For the Jesus who is transfigured, and for Luke who writes of him, such a transformed way of being belongs to every disciple, as both a privilege and an obligation.

Another transformative moment in Jesus' learning is reported in both Matthew and Mark. An outsider, a woman (identified as a "Gentile of Syrophoenician origin" in Mark), comes to Jesus when he is traveling in the Greek district of Tyre and Sidon. Matthew's version of the narrative highlights the drama: The woman kneels down before Jesus, begs for mercy, and tells him that her little daughter is possessed by a demon. Jesus ignores her. In effect, he conveys to the women, "you are invisible to me; you do not matter." Refusing to respond to someone who is addressing us, giving the person "the silent treatment," is cold and unkind. Psychologists consider it a form of emotional abuse. The scene could not be more poignant. A woman who already knows she is an outsider has swallowed her pride out of love for her child. She is in a position of supplication—on her knees! As the drama continues, the disciples of Jesus are equally callous: "Send her away, for she keeps shouting after us" (Mt 15:23). This hardly sounds like a response from those learning from the one who displays such compassion for the hurting crowds. A bewildering interaction between Jesus and the woman follows:

> "I was sent only to the lost sheep of the house of Israel."
> But she came and knelt before him, saying,
> "Lord, help me." He answered,
> "It is not fair to take the children's food and throw it to the dogs."
> She said, "Yes, Lord, yet even the dogs eat the crumbs
> that fall from their master's table."
> Then Jesus answered her, "Woman, great is your faith!
> Let it be done for you as you wish." (Mt 15:24–28)

Jesus is adamant in his belief that his ministry of healing belongs only to Israel. Since Gentiles are often called "dogs," there is a play on the word, which both Mark and Matthew soften to *kynarion* ("puppy"). Jesus says that he has not come to minister to the Gentiles. The woman's witty but polite reply does not directly contradict his perspective but offers Jesus some room to be more inclusive. She likens the Gentiles to the puppies that are allowed to eat crumbs that fall from the tables—the crumbs that would otherwise remain unused. Her image respects the tradition that Jews and Gentiles did not eat at the same table, while adding a pointed challenge. Surely, she suggests, there should be some leftover healing energy from Jesus that the Jews did not need. She would gladly accept it for her little daughter. Sometimes called the "uppity" woman of the gospels, this outsider has all the pluck, wisdom, and maternal love she needs to be a voice of healing. Highlighting her faith, the woman's daughter is pronounced healed, and Jesus moves on. Membership in the right group, the right religious tradition, or the right cultural background is not the criterion for receiving healing energy. The outsider has made her point. The narrative suggests that Jesus' attitude toward the outcast has changed. What would it take for such a transformation in attitude today toward all those considered strangers, unworthy, not welcome?

Who is transformed here? Is it Matthew's Jewish audience, who hears this story as a bristling challenge to be more inclusive? Is it other Gentiles, this woman's rejected companions, who rejoice in discovering that they too are included God's favor? Is it Jesus, who has to learn that all people are sons and daughters of a God who yearns to extend healing love to each of them? Since it is not the first time that Jesus is seen ministering among the Gentiles or emphasizing the wide-ranging embrace of God's reign in either Matthew or Mark, the narrative can also symbolize an earlier phase of Jesus' own developing awareness about the concept of inclusivity. Since his religious upbringing would have taught him about God's preference for Israel, this restrictive view had to be transformed. Somewhere early in his youthful journey did he see unrestrained love in a Gentile who would do anything for her child? Had it moved him, made him wonder? Was it a woman, a foreigner perhaps, who taught him about a God whose spacious love holds everyone in an immense universal embrace? Was it another dimension of his growth in wisdom and grace that culminated in the great transfiguration?

There is another message to examine in the narrative. "Send her away!" the disciples beg Jesus. Surely she had overstepped the bounds of propriety even in addressing him. Her persistence might have been annoying, a distraction to the real ministry at hand, or possibly an embarrassment. It was not the place of a woman, especially a Gentile, to speak to a man in public, much less with such determination.

"Send her away!" The request has a contemporary ring. Usher her back to her place in the background. Make her be quiet. Tell her to stop clamoring for power that is not rightfully hers. Such is the cry of patriarchy all over the world, both in cultures and in religious institutions that assign particular roles to women that hold less access to leadership than roles held by males. What is remarkable in the narrative is that Jesus listens to the woman's voice. He hears her wisdom and is changed by it. Could this be the greatest transformation of all?

TRANSFIGURATION TODAY

Transfiguration is not unique to Jesus. Neither is witnessing powerful change a prerogative of the disciples who knew the historical Jesus. All of us are called to go up the mountain, to climb the steep ground of truth where prejudices are identified, where the unexplored places of our souls are traversed, and where dormant possibilities of love are awakened. Transfiguration involves a lifetime journey. We go up the mountain of transformation accompanied by those closest to us, those who love us enough to challenge us. As we tell our deepest truth to someone, we become more transparent. The very process of interpersonal sharing, in a context of trust, makes us more radiant—revealing a brilliance that is numinous.

Psychology identifies mutual self-revelation with growth in human closeness. If I am closed to new experiences and ultra private about what I think and feel, I will have difficulty sustaining intimacy. Like light hidden under a bushel, I don't allow myself to be seen on the inside. Conversely, if I am open both to new experiences and to self-disclosure, I am more prepared to enter into life-giving friendships and relationships that last over time.

Transfiguration people are those who risk trudging up the often unpredictable topography of human interaction where control must be relinquished and the possibility of being changed is the only certainty. Transfiguration is ultimately about relationships where we are treated to little glimpses of one another's souls and come away awed by the sheer luminosity of the experience.

The same thing that awaited Jesus and his disciples in the mountain experience also awaits us. As friends and companions, community members and families, spouses and lovers, we accompany one another to a previously unseen place: I share a secret I have protected for too long. You show me your wounds. The mountain gets steeper, but we keep going, beginning to trust in this new path. We hear voices that sound like ours proclaiming revelation, pronouncing healing blessings that make their way into the marrow of our souls. Suddenly, when we least expect it, the light is brighter than we have ever known and words of belovedness penetrate our hearts. We want the moment to last forever, because we know instinctively that something powerful is happening. But we will inevitably journey back down the mountain to ordinary time, taking with us new clarity, and faces shining like the sun.

But we will come here again.

Chapter 8

Suffering

From Gethsemane to Golgotha

Then Jesus went with them to a place called Gethsemane;
and he said to his disciples, "Sit here while I go over there and pray."
He took with him Peter and the two sons of Zebedee,
And then began to be grieved and agitated.
And he said to them, "I am deeply grieved, even to death;
remain here, and stay awake with me."
And going on a little farther, he threw himself on the ground and
prayed,
"My Father, if it is possible, let this cup pass from me;
yet not what I want but what you want." (Mt 26:36–39)

He came out and went, as was his custom, to the Mount of Olives;
And the disciples followed him.
When he reached the place, he said to them,
"Pray that you may not come into the time of trial."
Then he withdrew from them about a stone's throw,
knelt down, and prayed, "Father, if you are willing, remove this cup
from me;
yet, not my will but yours be done."
When he got up from prayer, he came to the disciples
and found them sleeping because of grief, and he said to them,
"Why are you sleeping? Get up and pray that you may not come into
the time of trial." (Lk 22:39–46)

At three o'clock Jesus cried out with a loud voice,
"Eloi, Eloi, lema sabachthani?" which means,
"My God, My God, why have you forsaken me? ..."
Then Jesus gave a loud cry and breathed his last. (Mk 15:34, 37)

Then Jesus, crying out with a loud voice, said,
"Father, into your hands I commend my spirit."
Having said this, he breathed his last. (Lk 23:46)

When Jesus had received the wine, he said, "It is finished."
Then he bowed his head and gave up his spirit. (Jn 19:30)

It was the day we call Good Friday as the morning sun tried to break through the clouds—clouds that seemed determined to claim this day as theirs. He sat on a roughhewn wooden bench in the garden, his head in his hands, his grief raw. "He's so loving, so good. He's only thirty-one. I hoped he would have a few more years," he said of his only son. Hours later, when it was barely dawn on Easter Sunday morning, the young man who had inspired so many gave up his spirit. My brother, Robert, a faith-filled and generous man, would say later that afternoon that it was the worst day of his life. His words, from the foot of a cross freshly carved with his son Nathan's name on it, were a stark reminder that Good Friday and Easter Sunday are not two separate holy days. Gethsemane and the empty tomb are neighboring gardens.

Any parent who has lost a child knows well the terrain from Gethsemane to Golgotha. The fact that Nathan lost his battle with muscular dystrophy at age thirty-one, that he began the final leg of his particular way of the cross on Good Friday and died on Easter Sunday morning, did not ease the agony for his family. Comments from well-wishers about the beauty of dying on Easter fell flat. There was nothing beautiful in that moment in the Intensive Care Unit—only indescribable grief. The promise of Easter can never erase the agony that continues to dwell in the private crevices of the soul after such a Passover. Did the God that Jesus called Abba feel the same way at the suffering and death of his son? Was it the worst day of God's life when Jesus died?

IS THERE A GETHSEMANE GOD?

Posing such a question suggests that God can suffer. But how is this possible for the Supreme Being who painted the sky and gave each planet its personal orbit? If such a perfect creator is capable of feeling pain, why not do something to end it—for everyone? Such queries strike at the heart of how we understand God and how we grapple with one of life's most perplexing mysteries: suffering.

Using anthropomorphic language to talk about God is as common as reciting the Lord's Prayer. In the most popular translation, we address God as "Father," speak of "God's kingdom," and plead for favors, as if the holy one is endowed with male chromosomes, is CEO of a large piece of real estate, and receives requests like a divine Santa Claus—all of which make a caricature of the real meaning of the prayer Jesus gave his disciples.

Human qualities have long been assigned to God, most of which verify the stereotype of a male deity who governs from on high and rewards those who keep the rules. But if traditional theology and popular sentiment have wanted God to have human gender and an address in a place called heaven, both have been far less comfortable identifying other uniquely human characteristics with God—especially the capacity to experience suffering. Looking to art as one measure, God is often a white-skinned, older male with a soft beard and pleasant countenance who dwells near clouds. He might be portrayed as angry but never sad. Any hint of suffering in the Godhead is confined to Jesus, and then only on his way to Easter. Are the many forms of agony that are part of human life outside the experience of God? Does God grieve when people lose their battle with cancer, women are raped, or children starve to death in Darfur? Does God care if I hurt?

The notion of a God who is capable of suffering in response to human pain was not foreign to early philosophers and theologians, who grappled with the possibility of emotion in God in the first centuries of the church.[1] Until recent times theology viewed God as a supreme monarch who remains unmoved and unchanging—a teaching protected by the Council of Chalcedon in 451: "The synod deposes from the priesthood those who dare to say that the Godhead of the only-begotten is passible."[2] While this depiction of God protects the "otherness" of the deity, it ignores a preponderance of metaphors of a compassionate God in the bible as well as the fact that emotionally charged and suffering humans are said to have been made in this God's image (Gn 1:27). It also suggests an inflated confidence within the church about its own pronouncements.

The question of suffering in God has changed today because it has been increasingly impossible to reconcile a God who *cares* with a God who is *unaffected* by human pain. Although theological literature by the early twentieth century shows a growing reaction against a remote, unfeeling God, it was the reality of the Holocaust that brought about a rediscovery of "a God deeply involved with the pain of the world."[3] The unthinkable horror of this event shook the very foundations of whatever belief remained in a divine being who was impassible—who could stand aloof while millions were systematically exterminated like bothersome rodents. Could this not qualify as another worst day of God's life?

In response to the terrible realities of genocide, as well as other occasions of human agony, theology has looked again and found a Gethsemane God—a divine being that abhors the cross but will not leave anyone hanging there alone. It has been said that whatever agony makes its way into the human spirit, God's is the first heart to be broken.[4] Such an understanding of God ought not only console us but also change us.

TENDING THE GARDEN OF GETHSEMANE

Clearly, mainstream theology has committed itself to a God who is affected by human pain while, at the same time, maintaining diverse opinions about the precise nature of God's involvement in suffering.[5] While many contemporary theologians have articulated powerful insights about the God who feels the weight of every cross, Johann Baptist Metz argues that a "suffering God" can too easily cause us to over-spiritualize the reality of evil endured by victims.[6] His point is not that God is indifferent to human suffering, but rather, that the question of human suffering should remain out in the open where the promise of resurrection ought never silence the cry from the cross.[7] Metz's plea to keep the face of suffering before us is an effort to stir us to action—to do whatever we can in solidarity with victims to work for justice and healing in their memory.

Any attempt to resolve the mystery of human agony with a final rationale would, for Metz and many other theologians, relieve us from the responsibility to continue to wrestle with its multiple causes. A primary outcome of a theology of suffering is not to *explain* it but to assist in discerning when it is caused by human violence or ignorance, and when it is, act forcefully to eliminate it.

History has a way of nudging us forward more deeply into the mystery of God, forcing us to take our previously answered questions back to the messy and distressing places of life where God never finishes speaking, calling, loving, suffering. Belief in a God who is unmoved by human suffering gives *us* permission to remain unaffected by it as well. We can keep our distance, protecting ourselves from knowing too much about war zones, killing fields, refugee camps, and garbage dumps where children exchange play for scavenging. I can avoid the hospital rooms where the rattle of last breaths makes me queasy. If God sinks into the impassive distance that protects against pain, and compels no intervention, so can I. But a God who suffers at the plight of suffering humanity changes things. If God is there, how can I justify leaving? If God is intimately involved in the anguish of the world, all believers are called to be there as well. Wherever human pain is found, it enters into the compassionate heart of God, who shares it, feels it, and asks that we do the same. Even Jesus did not enter Gethsemane alone.

REMOVE THIS CUP

It is the most common prayer in the midst of suffering: Remove this cup. Let it pass me by. Take away the pain. Make it different.

There are so many ways to beg God to intervene and change the outcome of suffering: Please let him recover. Make her get well. Help us get through this. Don't let this divorce happen. Even those who claim to be nonbelievers can suddenly lapse into desperate pleas to a deity they are not sure they believe in when the cup of suffering is held to their lips. It is unlikely that anyone who suffers does so without wondering if there is some way for the cup to pass by, this time.

This illustrates one of the many paradoxes inherent in suffering—what is its source? What power does the sufferer have to remove or overcome it? What about human suffering from war, hunger, genocide, violence, disease? Not all roads from Gethsemane need inevitably lead to Golgotha.

The first question I must ask in any garden called Gethsemane has to do with the nature of the cup. Can it be removed? Jesus is not above pondering the normal human question of escape from suffering that occurs to everyone facing pain. Is there a secret way out of this garden, a back path that will allow me to avoid the cross and still hold my integrity intact? Was that his real agony? Is he asking *God* to take away the dreaded cup, or asking *himself* if he really has to drink it?

This is also our question in the midst of suffering. Is the source of pain an inevitable part of human frailty that we are helpless to reverse, or is it rooted in human failure that could be set right? With some types of suffering there is a point of no return. Everything possible has been done to treat an illness, to resolve a conflict, to address whatever brokenness has fractured the body or the heart. Other times, suffering has found its way in through a giant fissure in the integrity of a person or a nation. It has been given permission to settle in and stay, not because there is nothing we can do to end it, but because the anguish of a person or the torture of a whole group serves the collective interest of someone who has decided that the suffering has a sordid benefit for some. It is a sad irony that economically developed countries have often turned their backs on atrocities taking place in poorer nations that have no wealth to offer.

That is called social sin, institutionalized evil. Fighting it is ultimately what kills Jesus. He persists in giving full voice to his convictions about God's reign. He condemns the structures of injustice in both the civil government and in the religious institution of his day, advocating an open table and an end to the greed that keeps the peasant population downtrodden. His criticism of the rigidity of the religious leaders is not born of hostility to authority, but of a disdain for the pompous righteousness they exhibit as they burden the people with superficial laws and exclude anyone who does not fit their idea of perfection. Jesus fights this brand of hypocrisy, and it costs him dearly.

When a cross is built of hatred, intolerance, violence, greed, or any one of a number of other human vices, theology's task is neither to explain the pain nor soothe the suffering, especially for those who have power to do something about it. In the presence of this kind of suffering we cannot excuse ourselves from action by citing some form of the often misunderstood words of Jesus about the poor (or the "other") always being with us (Mt 26:11). Looking at his ministry in context, should we not be asking other questions: Why are some of those who are with us poor? Why are some of them starving? Why are there refugees among us, driven from their land? Why do some of those who are with us have no clean water or medical care? Why do some die of preventable diseases? Along with a theology to help us understand how God is present in the suffering of the victims of collective sin, we also need one that helps us understand how we are to be present to them to eliminate the causes of their agony. This is what incarnation demands. But delving into the entire paschal mystery is not easy. Sleeping through Good Friday—closing our eyes to injustice—at least allows some of us to make it to Easter, or does it?

STAY AWAKE

Jesus' words to his disciples in Gethsemane offer a biblical stance toward suffering. "Remain here and stay awake with me" (Mt 26:38). These words, pleas really, find their way to most of our lips as we undergo the loneliness of a dreaded ordeal ahead: Stay a little longer. Please don't go yet. I can't be alone right now. This is Jesus at his most human, and perhaps his most divine— divinity is about being present in love. Throughout his life, Jesus feels the continuous presence of the one he calls Abba. Here, he seeks that same kind of holy presence from those who are closest to him. "Stay awake with me." The words that come to us from Matthew's gospel suggest that Jesus plans to stay awake himself— to remain fully present to his hour—to feel it, even to embrace it. But he does not want to do it alone.

Much suffering that erupts into our lives and disrupts our sleep at night has its source in limitations of the human condition—we will all eventually die, and when we do, someone will grieve. The best theologizing, the most sophisticated psychological theories, cannot offer an explanation that removes the pain of it. There are illnesses and accidents, losses and disappointments, failures and finalities that no good behavior on our part or courageous acts of justice on the part of others can prevent: My mother de- velops congestive heart failure for which there is no treatment. My teenager is in an ATV accident that puts him in a year-long coma before it takes his life. I fail to get a promotion because someone else is more qualified. A tornado takes the roof off our home. It is in response to these forms of suffering that good the- ology and psychology can help, not to purge pain from our lives, but to offer us a way to carry it. Crying, praying, staying involved can all help, but it is the human *presence* of a caring relationship that most sustains us through painful times.

Traversing the terrain of the garden of agony is not comfort- able. Who would choose to go there, except a loved one accom- panying a child, a spouse, or a friend whose destiny was this final place of suffering? Do any of us feel at home in Gethsemane? It is hardly a destination of choice. Usually, we want to move on, to get out of the infamous garden as quickly as possible, and we want grief-stricken family and friends to leave with us. Most of us have heard pious attempts to dull the voice of suffering after a death: "She's in a better place." "At least he didn't linger." "Their suffering is over now." Such platitudes offer comfort aimed less at the victim or the loved ones and more toward those of us who cannot bear to stay awake to their pain. Unbearable grief cries out for relief, for numbness. Like the disciples in Gethsemane, we can only take so much sadness. Often, sleep is a way out—either physically or metaphorically—as unwelcome pain settles in. If sleep does not come easily for our bodies, we can put our awareness to sleep, anesthetizing it with hollow sentiments that dull its intensity.

It is normal, of course, to comfort ourselves and others at times of great sorrow with words that fit the truth of the situation. I still remind myself that my parents, who died in their nineties, lived good and long lives—messages that my siblings and I heard countless times at our parents' funerals. But that does not take away the sense of loss or justify their final suffering. There is nothing that allows me to think that their suffering made perfect sense. That it was inevitable, yes. That it was necessary, no. There is still a "why" that lives on in me. For theologian Jürgen Moltmann, each innocent sufferer, "like Job, indignantly rejects any religious explanations of why he or she must suffer."[8] Human attempts to *explain* the reasons for suffering can give it license, legitimizing its power to inflict pain. Most of the time, what you and I need in the wake of suffering is presence—someone to be with us, quietly understanding the agony and not offering devout remarks to validate its presence.

"Stay awake with me." These words of Jesus are a powerful mandate. More than just a personal request they can be heard as an urgent appeal in behalf of all of those whose plights have taken them to a place called Gethsemane, or intensive care, or death row, or a tent city after a natural disaster. Stay awake! Look around! See! Feel the fear. Don't leave anyone alone in this dreaded place. Smell the garbage. See the vacant eyes. Hear the despair. Stay awake with them.

Staying awake has both past and present implications, and personal and communal dimensions. Not only does it involve remaining present to those who currently suffer, including ourselves, but it also calls upon all of us to stay awake to the suffering of the world, to never forget the atrocities that have been perpetrated on innocent people in the past. Theologian Johann Baptist Metz refers to this act of staying awake as one of the essential responses to human suffering. He calls it "remembering."[9] It is in remembering that future suffering can be diminished and other genocides might be prevented. Inherently eucharistic, as Elizabeth Johnson points out, remembering helps us stay affectively connected to the people and events that need our continued involvement.[10] If we remember, we will feel. If we feel, we are more likely to act.

In Washington DC at the Holocaust Museum there is a huge boxcar with an open top. It is the musty smell that announces its poignant contents even before the car is visible. Then, as eyes slowly become accustomed to the dimly lit space and dare to look down, there they are: the shoes. The boxcar is full of them— thousands of scruffy oxfords, dirty sandals, broken high heels. It is the tiny baby shoes, scattered among the symbols of lives stopped dead in their tracks, that cry out with an anguish that could not but help break God's heart. As women and men of all ages, races, and abilities file gingerly along the walkway, peering down into the box car that reeks of agony, most fall silent. Some hold onto each other as if to grasp a bit of life in this place that holds too much death. A few utter barely audible gasps of horror as the stark reality of evil stares up at them. The last time I visited this place of remembrance, a young man in a military uniform knelt down and sobbed. An older woman with damp eyes gently touched his shoulder, waiting there with him until he could move on. She said nothing. Perhaps this is how God responds to human suffering: Touching. Waiting. Being there. Speechless. Could it be that sometimes God doesn't know what to say to ease the pain? Could God's silence feel like God's absence?

Memory holds reality for us. It stores all of the sights, sounds, smells, and feelings that have accumulated in our personal and collective histories, all of the people and events that we dare not forget lest we lose our way. Memory is the inner vision of the past that connects us to the truth of our lives and clears a path for the future. The Holocaust Memorial stands in service of human memory as one way to honor its victims and provide them a home in time. But perhaps more important, it binds the horrors of that carnage to our minds so we will not allow its wretched evil to be repeated.

In simple gestures of remembrance, we have begun to display our causes and concerns with ribbons and wristbands—tangible evidence of what we are committed to keeping close to our hearts. Yellow ribbons tied around a tree in the late 1970s came to symbolize hostages held in Iran. In 1990–91 the yellow ribbons represented soldiers returning from the first Iraq war. Today colored wristbands and lapel ribbons, large and small, symbolize numerous causes: red is for AIDS/HIV and Mothers Against Drunk Driving; orange represents world hunger and agent orange exposure; yellow stands for POW/MIA; green for Save Darfur; blue for child abuse prevention; purple for the victims of 9/11 and for the homeless; lime green calls to mind muscular dystrophy. White is for Holocaust remembrance. At first glance, wearing a colored ribbon or wristband might seem a small and ineffectual act. But little things often have a way of evoking recognition. If we can remember, even for a few moments, we might remain unsettled enough to act for justice in behalf of at least one cause.

A GOD WHO REMEMBERS

There is biblical precedent for remembering. When the people complain that God has forsaken them, Isaiah offers a tender reminder of God's continual presence:

> *Can a woman forget her nursing child,*
> *or show no compassion for the child of her womb?*
> *Even these may forget, yet I will not forget you. (Is 49:15)*

The God of the bible is a God of remembering, a maternal God who stays as absorbed in the care of her child as does a nursing mother. The cry of the people that elicited Isaiah's message is a refrain that resounds through the ages: "The Lord has forsaken me, my Lord has forgotten me" (Is 49:14). Like the Israelites feeling forsaken by God, you and I know the profound sense of God's absence that can accompany suffering when it enters our lives. Even though I cling to a persistent hope that a God of goodness can relieve pain, cure diseases, stop holocausts, and halt crucifixions, I begin to wonder if God is still there when suffering continues or death is not prevented. Even Jesus sounded the cry of the abandoned as he hung on his particular cross.

The haunting words of Isaiah promise no release from suffering—just a nursing presence in its midst. God deals with suffering humanity by *remembering*, by being a nursing mother who never leaves her child. The reality of this holy presence is not dependent on my ability to feel it, nor is it confirmed by easing my pain.

Have you ever stood by in agony, helpless to stop the anguish of someone you love? In its own incomprehensible way such an experience speaks about how God suffers. We know that an infant absorbed in nursing makes no distinction between itself and the nourishing breast of its mother. But if the flow of milk stops before hunger has been satisfied, the wail of abandonment commences.

Isaiah's image of God as a remembering mother offers a metaphor for how God is present to suffering. When I am comfortable, when things are going well, I can be like the satisfied child at the breast—not immediately conscious of the ultimate source of fullness in my life. But when I am in pain, my awareness is jarred. I become more focused on the absence of comfort. Pain, particularly when it is intense, has a way of seizing my attention, pulling me away from everything but my distress. A sense of absence is my first response to suffering. The same maternal presence is there, even though I am unable to feel it. Was it that way for Jesus—a least for a moment?

"Eloi, Eloi, lema sabachthani?" (Mk 15:34). By whatever name we know God, the message in the cry from the cross is universal—it is the sense of being left alone, forgotten at a time of greatest need. "My God, My God, why have you forsaken me?" The cry of Jesus has been uttered in every language and in every location of suffering the world over. From emergency rooms and burn units to the trenches of war and the gutters of the ghetto, the words have been wailed and whimpered, scribbled on walls and scratched on prison-cell bars. Picasso immortalized them on canvas in his painting "Guernica," where stricken faces scream the words from the cross in silent horror. The body count from the Inquisition overshadows the single killing of Matthew Shepard, and one person's death in a car accident pales in comparison to the massive loss of life in a plane crash. But however large or small the resulting grief, it is hard to imagine God being indifferent to the suffering of any one of them. A single death moves the heart of God—a truth I cannot confirm but only trust.

WHY JESUS DIED

In the end, Jesus was not in Gethsemane headed toward Golgotha because God needed a perfect human sacrifice to make up for the sin of humankind. Only a sadistic deity would require the death of anyone, much less a beloved child. All his life he had addressed God as Abba ("Papa")—which we can also understand as "Mama"—the one who took absolute delight in a child born of love.

The notion that God *sent* Jesus to die to atone for human sin is an unfortunate and damaging distortion of the mystery of incarnation, one that biblical scholars are increasingly addressing and correcting.[11] Aside from bad soteriology (the study of doctrines of salvation), interpreting the crucifixion of Jesus as a sacrifice for human sin that was *required by God* endows suffering with religious rationale that is abusive, putting pressure on the sufferer to accept even those conditions of pain that ought to be rejected with Job's fierceness. Too often the promise of a heavenly reward has been used to manipulate acceptance of the injustices of poverty, inequality, and violence. In the 1990s in Guatemala the military inundated the indigenous poor with messages over loudspeakers glorifying suffering, encouraging the poor to welcome affliction on earth in order to earn a higher place in heaven. The aim was to squelch resistance. There was nothing holy about this victimization.

There is yet another serious danger in any theory of atonement that validates the violence of the crucifixion by claiming it was needed to assuage God's wrath: it legitimizes parental mistreatment of children. Increasingly understood as divine child abuse, older atonement theories present as normal a father's right to subject a child to cruel punishment or sanction a primitive paternal thirst for revenge for a child's disobedience. Too many parents take out their anger on their children as it is, and they don't need a religious image to justify their brutality.

Jesus *did* die because of sin, but not because God needed or wanted a perpetuation of senseless scapegoat violence. Jesus was murdered because his preaching about love and his healing embrace of all was perceived as too great a threat to a civil and religious establishment that sought to maintain control over wealth and truth. He died for the same reason that many prophets die— they touch a nerve that others do not want touched. But there was a difference between the death of Jesus and that of other prophetic leaders: no one responded to the crucifixion of Jesus with further violence. No one was hunted down, imprisoned, or executed for killing him. With his nonviolent response to violence came a brief respite in retribution. He was not willing to return violence with violence. Neither were his followers in the immediate aftermath of his death.

All four evangelists report that it was a violent, armed mob that came to arrest Jesus in the garden of Gethsemane. The chief priests and officers of the Temple police were part of the crowd bearing swords and clubs that swarmed into the garden where olive trees grew and one lone man of remarkable courage posed too much of a threat to the civil and religious status quo to let him slip away. The overreaction of the wild scene did not escape the notice of Jesus: "Have you come out with swords and clubs to arrest me as though I were bandit?" (Mt 26:55). Jesus talked to violence. He spoke the truth to it. But he did not return it.

BECOMING THE PASCHAL MYSTERY

Suffering comes in many forms. Jesus did not suffer and die because of illness, accident, old age, or any natural cause. His life and death reflect the kind of suffering that comes from steadfastly refusing any claim of privilege or prestige, embodying God's liberating love in his being, and calling upon all of his followers to do the same. The gospels record his relentless path toward Jerusalem, and the inevitability of the cross, as Jesus held true to his vision and purpose. Anyone who opposes the controlling powers of any group or institution will meet a cross—a cross of rejection and hatred that is sometimes strong enough to kill.

As Jesus moves about the area, attracting attention for his teaching and healing, angering some and inspiring others, the tension mounts and resentment against him builds. It isn't just that he is an *individual* itinerant preacher or worker of miracles—that would have been far less threatening. Jesus' real danger to the establishment is his conviction that all the people had power within to heal, to love, to overcome inequality and poverty.

What would happen if he succeeded in convincing everyone to set the captives free or proclaim the Lord's year of favor? In rejecting the messianic role for himself, Jesus "seems to have been moving messiahship from its projection onto public leaders, however great, to an inner reality whose latent powers everyone must discover for themselves."[12] In other words, Jesus has so profoundly internalized a sense of God's way that he comes to personify holiness. Even more, he wants each of us to discover within ourselves what he has found. He is saying, by his actions, that it is the responsibility of all of us to address the evils and pain of the people, and that we have the collective power to do it. Both the essence and the secret of messianic energy are that this power is available to everyone—we are all are called to save, to heal, and to proclaim God's reign:

> *Then Jesus called the twelve together*
> *and gave them power and authority over all the demons*
> *and to cure diseases,*
> *and he sent them out to proclaim the kingdom of God*
> *and to heal. (Lk 9:1–2)*

The disciples are on a roll. They believe in themselves and in the power of the holy within them, and they go "through the villages, bringing the good news and curing diseases everywhere"

(Lk 9:6). "The Lucan theme of universalism sounds forth."[13] The disciples go "everywhere"—no one is left out. Jesus' vision is one where the most wounded are the most welcome. Those most left out are now in charge of the guest list for the banquet. Good news and healing belong to all.

This is a dangerous vision to take seriously. Laden with potential suffering for those who believe it and dare to live it, it is not surprising that consistent efforts have been made to water it down and reduce it to superficial laws that religious establishments can monitor. No wonder Herod the ruler was perplexed when he heard about such a free-wheeling dispensation of grace (Lk 9:7). He had executed John the Baptist. Now Herod's power and authority were jeopardized again. This is the insidious seed of the kind of torment Jesus faced—someone with power feels threatened by fear of its diminishment. The stage for suffering is set. Props for a crucifixion must be put in place.

Later in Luke's gospel Jesus again encourages his disciples to act with holy authority when the Twelve come to him because the crowd that has followed them is hungry. Again, Jesus suggests that they have the power themselves to feed the people:

> The twelve came to him and said,
> "Send the crowd away, so that they may go into the
> surrounding villages and countryside,
> to lodge and get provisions; for we are here in a deserted place."
> But he said to them,
> "You give them something to eat." (Lk 9:12–13)

You feed them. You find the food. You set the table. The command is crystal clear. In Jesus' way of understanding God's reign, no one who is hungry should be sent away, and those who see the hunger have the responsibility to find the resources. Once again, the disciples are surprised by their ability to meet the needs of the community—to prepare a banquet where everyone is filled. In the reign of God a few loaves and a couple of fish are blessed and become a blessing for all. The background of the story is important—people traveled with crusts of bread and dried fish hidden in the folds of their garments. Here, the disciples encouraged all of the people to share what they had, so that those who lacked provisions could eat. This is true ministry. It is also good politics. And it is a real miracle. How many baskets would be left over today if those who had access to beans and rice opened their pocketbooks, or their banks, for those who are starving? *You* feed them! Really? How seriously should we take such an outlandish command? Why not reduce this unrealistic saying to a metaphor and leave the miracles to Jesus?

It is shortly after this in the Lucan narrative that Jesus tells his disciples that he must undergo great suffering, be rejected by the religious leaders, and be killed. Biblical suffering happens whenever anyone takes the reign of God so seriously that those who stand to lose control are threatened. For the followers of Jesus, for you and for me, feeding the hungry, healing the sick, and gathering in all those who are left out are the risky tasks of discipleship. Doing so is a sacrificial way of life that is destined to infuriate those who wish to cling to power and control and who know that gains for the destitute and newly empowered will be their loss.

Chapter 9

Easter

Proclaiming Resurrection

When the sabbath was over,
Mary Magdalene, and Mary the mother of James,
and Salome brought spices, so that they might go and anoint him.
And very early on the first day of the week, when the sun had risen,
they went to the tomb. . . .
When they looked up, they saw that the stone, which was very large,
had already been rolled back.
As they entered the tomb, they saw a young man,
dressed in a white robe,
sitting on the right side; and they were alarmed.
But he said to them, "Do not be alarmed;
you are looking for Jesus of Nazareth, who was crucified.
He has been raised; he is not here." (Mk 16:1–2, 4–6)

After the sabbath, as the first day of the week was dawning,
Mary Magdalene and the other Mary went to see the tomb.
And suddenly there was a great earthquake;
for an angel of the Lord, descending from heaven,
came and rolled back the stone and sat on it. . . .
The angel said to the women, "Do not be afraid;
I know that you are looking for Jesus who was crucified.
He is not here;
for he has been raised, as he said." (Mt 28:1–2, 5–6)

145

But on the first day of the week, at early dawn,
they came to the tomb,
taking the spices that they had prepared.
They found the stone rolled away from the tomb,
but when they went in, they did not find the body.
While they were perplexed about this,
suddenly two men in dazzling white clothes stood beside them.
The women were terrified and bowed their faces to the ground,
but the men said to them,
"Why do you look for the living among the dead?
He is not here, but has risen." (Lk 24:1–5)

Early on the first day of the week, while it was still dark,
Mary Magdalene came to the tomb
and saw that the stone had been removed from the tomb. (Jn 20:1)

Mary Magdalene went and announced to the disciples,
"I have seen the Lord";
and she told them that he had said these things to her. (Jn 20:18)

AN EMPTY TOMB

Early in the morning after my mother died, I went to the funeral home, taking with me the clothes my siblings and I had prepared for her burial. I hoped that being there, near her body, would bring me a sense of her presence. A kind young man dressed in a suit and tie met me and made every effort to be comforting. But it didn't feel like Easter. All I remember is the emptiness—my mother wasn't there.

The empty tomb stories were written to encourage faith in the resurrection for Christians who had not known the historical Jesus—and that includes each of us. But in addition to proclaiming resurrection, these narratives give tangible reality to the bleakness that follows death. When someone we love dies, moving from desolation to resurrection takes time. Initially, grief claims every space in our heart. We all experience this journey from death to life uniquely, and few of us describe it exactly the same way after some time has passed. Yet studies point to a universal experience of emptiness at the beginning. The first disciples of Jesus were no different. They looked back on his death in deeply personal ways and told stories to convey the impact it made on their lives. For all of them it started with emptiness—a tomb that no longer held the person they had known.

HE IS RISEN

Christians today would be in trouble if Easter faith depended on synonymous accounts of the resurrection. Mindful of the needs of their particular communities, the evangelists rely on inspiration within as they edit and shape the ancient oral accounts of Easter faith they had inherited. Just as one artist's painting of the resurrection cannot be superimposed on others, gospel works of art are not intended to be merged into a single story with all parts fitting logically together. Each inspired account carries imagery that leads us closer to the unfathomable mystery of Easter. Interpretation that allows for spiritual creativity is less tidy and will undoubtedly leave many questions unanswered, but Easter faith is more at home in the soil of trust. If all facts could be been verified, and all questions answered, we would have no need for Easter *faith*.

Although "no two resurrection accounts in the four Gospels are alike," and all "seem to be late additions to the tradition,"[1] the women and men who knew Jesus of Nazareth and accompanied him to the end experienced something that has been remembered for two thousand years. Even though exact recall of details faded and various accounts of his life and death conflicted with one another, the *impact* that Jesus made intensified and expanded over time—*this* is the essential truth of resurrection. After his death his influence increased.

Whatever happened after the crucifixion, his followers came to know with an assurance called *faith* that Jesus was still with them. In some mysterious way he had risen—risen in their hearts, risen in their lives, and was now closer to them than their heartbeat, nearer than their breath. He lived in them. As they shared their new experiences of him with one another, their conviction of his continuing presence grew. Private spiritual experience burst forth in shared Easter faith. Yes, they had all *seen him*. He had risen as he said. They were sure of it.

Talking about Easter faith is no easier for us than it was for the first disciples. We cannot prove our faith with words—each time we describe how we have met God in our lives, the narrative falls short of conveying both the reality and emotional depth of our experience. Resurrection is just one incident that is implanted in a series of sacred mysteries that cannot be easily explained or separated one from the other. Although Christians celebrate resurrection as a feast on Easter Sunday, the entire paschal mystery comes along. Suffering and death are contiguous to resurrection. Gethsemane and Golgotha linger in the shadows as dawn breaks on Easter morning. Though not defined as part of the paschal mystery, there is a relationship among all spiritual events that are counted as feast days on the Christian calendar. Easter is irrevocably bound to annunciation. Visitation and incarnation inhabit its history. The paschal mystery is planted in the sands of the wilderness experience and prefigured in the transfiguration. We are immersed into the mystery of all of it at our baptism. Easter, like other spiritual happenings in our lives, cannot exist in isolation. It is called a *feast* because it requires company.

Easter is the energy of the holy as it is nurtured in human experience. Easter energy cannot be confined to a tomb or narrated in a single story. Impatient to erupt into actions that heal and words that inspire goodness, the energy of Easter is like a sacred earthquake that shakes the foundations of doubt, leaving little the same in the heart of the seeker. It bursts forth in our lives whenever stones of fear and doubt are rolled away so new life can emerge.

EASTER WOMEN

All of the resurrection narratives are introduced by the same figure—Mary of Magdala. Mary is an icon of devoted attendance, of love that stays. Her presence is so strongly associated with the crucifixion-resurrection tradition that all four evangelists, in an unusual convergence of detail, state that she was the first to go to the tomb. Did she go with spices to anoint the body of Jesus, as Mark and Luke report, or did she go to grieve, just to be near him, as Matthew and John suggest? Was she alone or with other women? Was it daylight or dark? However divergent the details, Mary of Magdala was a main player in the early Christian community.

Unmistakably a woman of extraordinary determination and leadership, Mary Magdalen performed a most central role in the birth of Christianity. "Without her courageous initiative and witness and that of the 'many other women' (Mark 15:41) with her, there would be no continuity in the story surrounding the end of Jesus' life, no paschal narrative."[2] In fact, if Mary Magdalen and the other women had been as silenced in the resurrection accounts as she and they have been in later Christianity, our Easter stories would indeed be spare.

Given the patriarchal context of the times, it is remarkable that we have these stories at all—that all four gospel writers chronicled one singular woman's prominence in the pivotal launch of Christianity while specifically stating that most of the male disciples had fled the gruesome crucifixion scene. At the Easter vigil, again on Easter Sunday, and on several days during the octave of Easter, the stories of the steadfast faith of these women are proclaimed during the liturgy. Mary Magdalen and the women who stayed at the cross and went to the tomb were the first to know of the resurrection, to announce it, to lead us to Easter. How ironic that their Catholic sisters cannot proclaim these gospel stories at liturgical celebrations today precisely because they are women! Given their crucial initial influence, only a radical departure from the practice and attitude of Jesus and the early church can explain the absence of women in leadership and sacramental ministry in Catholic Christianity today.

A GARDENER GOD

It makes sense that Mary saw the newly risen One as a gardener. He was, after all, made in the image of the God who had fashioned the first humans and set them in a garden. Jesus had incarnated the God of Eden. He had likened the reign of God to seed and talked of vineyards, plants, and different kinds of soil. Tilling and keeping (Gn 2:15) were in his soul—surely he would be at home in a garden. And the garden called Gethsemane—he had just been there.

"Woman, why are you weeping? Whom are you looking for?" (Jn 20:15). These are paschal mystery questions addressed to each of us. But like anyone who has just experienced the death of a loved one, Mary's anguish is still too deep for casual visiting, much less pondering resurrection mysteries. Her heart can only handle more practical concerns. In a courteous but decisive display of authority, she tells the gardener-God that she will take the body of Jesus away if he will tell her where he has carried him—if indeed he has.

Beneath Mary's search for a corpse is a far more salient quest: Where is he? Now that he is dead, where has he gone? What remains? The searing sense of absence after a death creates a vacuum that aches to be filled—maybe if she can see him one more time, touch his body, her pain will ease for a moment. Mary of Magdala symbolizes all of us who are suspended in that agonizing place between Good Friday and Easter Sunday when we cannot quite comprehend either the reality or magnitude of our loss. Mary believes in the charismatic carpenter whose ministry she shared, whose love she knew, but she is yet to come to Easter faith. Jesus has died. His body is gone. She has not experienced his risen presence in a decisive way. Her search for the missing body of Jesus is a pursuit of resolution after his death. In her name and ours, Mary of Magdala is seeking resurrection.

How often do we miss the revelation of the holy because ordinariness gets in its way? Our expectations prevent us from seeing beyond what is right before our eyes. A death is literally the end. Grief looms so large that it trumps any hope of future joy. A gardener is just a gardener. What we see immediately before us is all we see. The question, "Whom are you looking for?" is easily postponed. It is possible to live our entire lives in spiritual limbo—hanging in suspense between the sorrow we know and the risen life that we cannot possibly imagine. That is how it was for Mary of Magdala in the immediate aftermath of the immense torrent of sorrow that washed over her heart. Do you recognize it? Eventually, she hears him say her name. "Mary!" (Jn 20:16). A simple acknowledgment of her presence, recognition that she was there was enough. He says her name. In naming Mary, he names every woman who has been left out, made anonymous, ignored. Then, a most incredible thing happens: He tells her to "go to my brothers and say to them, 'I am ascending to my Father and your Father, to my God and your God'" (Jn 20:17). He commissions her, a woman, to be the first to announce the resurrection. In a remarkable twist of patriarchal protocol, she, a woman, will proclaim to the men. In a narrative that conveys Mary of Magdala's importance in the early Christian community, she carries her newfound Easter faith to the disciples. "I have seen the Lord" (Jn 2:18), she says simply. Though attempts will be made through the ages to blunt her voice, to forget her name, and to discredit her person, her story is recorded, and Christians of all generations hear it and come to a greater trust of their own.

COMING TOWARD EASTER FAITH

After the crucifixion of Jesus the community of disciples was devastated. It took them time to regroup, to recognize that Jesus was still with them, that his spirit was in them in all of its power. The gospels record their gradual journey toward Easter faith using symbols, stories, and words that are uncommon: *resurrection, ascension,* and *pentecost.* Inseparable from the crucifixion, they are all part of the great passing over from death to life. On the journey that transports each of us toward Easter faith, we too experience the same dying and rising in the mystery we call paschal. We *pass over*, tumbling from death to numbness, numbness to grief, grief to anger, anger to a quiet dawn of something brighter— we hear our name in a new way, and suddenly it is Easter.

In John's gospel Thomas is an example of one who transitioned through various levels of Easter faith (Jn 20:24–28). Remembered for his initial doubt, he comes to symbolize anyone who is moved to believe as a result of an encounter with the risen Lord. Thomas has often served as an example of weak faith or stubborn resistance to believe. His words can sound defiant: "Unless I see the mark of the nails in his hands, and put my finger in the mark of the nails and my hand in his side, I will not believe" (Jn 20:25). Symbolic of each of us at times of intractable doubt, Thomas insists on getting proof, tangible verification that Jesus, the one who had been crucified, now lives. He wants to see physical signs and touch evidence with his own hands or he will not believe. When Jesus finally stands in their midst and offers Thomas the chance, Thomas says simply: "My Lord and my God!" (Jn 20:28). His faith, though late in blooming, culminates in "the highest Christological confession in the gospels."[3] In the end, Thomas is not moved to faith because of proof—the story suggests that he never actually touches Jesus. He doesn't need tangible evidence any longer because something else, something that transcends proof, has taken place in him. He believes because he sees in a new way. He sees from the inside, with eyes of faith. It is this kind of faith that evaporates the need for literal confirmation.

The story of Thomas is neither an account of faith in particular teachings nor human substantiation of facts. It is about personal intimacy with the wounds of the risen One. It is interesting that Thomas, in an earlier stage of coming to believe, did not simply want to *see Jesus* with his own eyes. He specifically wanted to see his *wounds*, and beyond seeing them, he wanted to *touch* them. Without realizing it at the time, Thomas understands that it is often in seeing and touching wounds, both our own and those of others, that brings us into contact with the holy. When Francis of Assisi finally brings himself to touch the sores of a leper, he comes face to face with God, and it transforms him forever.

John is writing for Christians who, like Thomas, were finding it difficult to believe that Jesus had risen, since they had no tangible proof of it. "Blessed are you who have not seen yet have come to believe" (Jn 20:29), the Johannine Jesus says. He seems to be reaching out from within the narrative to those Christians in John's time, and ours, who need encouragement in their faith. In the story Jesus recognizes that Easter faith does not happen in one dramatic moment. Those who "have come to believe" are blessed—those who need time, who have doubts, whose progress toward Easter is as precarious as the way of the cross. Blessed are they who limp to Easter, who move toward it with hesitation. Blessed are they who need a Veronica to comfort them, and a Simon of Cyrene to lift them up when their steps falter. Blessed are they who gather up their reservations and skepticisms and keep going. Blessed are they who eventually recognize him when a stranger stands before them and shows them his wounds. "My Lord and my God!" Such certainty of faith is often slow in coming. Who knew this better than the disciples on the road to Emmaus?

STAY WITH US

The loss had been too much for them. They were leaving, fleeing Jerusalem with all its violence and death, and going home. Cleopas and his companion, believed by some scholars to be his wife, were walking the seven miles back to Emmaus (Lk 24:13–35). Not unlike discouraged modern-day disciples it looked as though not much good had come out of their early belief in Jesus or their enthusiasm for his mission. They were like disheartened believers today whose faith has been affected by the dismantling of Vatican II or shaken by the widespread coverup of clergy sexual abuse. Cleopas and his companion were sincere followers whose trust had fallen victim to hopelessness and to structures of control and injustice erected in the name of God.

When the long Lucan narrative begins, the journey to Emmaus is hardly one of faith. These were disciples who had known Jesus, traveled with him, heard him teach, seen him heal the sick, yet none of it had been enough to move them to Easter faith after the devastation of the past few days—a comforting thing, perhaps, for contemporary Christians to remember. Yes, they had heard the stories of the women who had been to the tomb that very morning and claimed to have seen a vision of angels who said he was alive. Some of their company had gone to see for themselves, looking for Jesus, "but they did not see him" (Lk

24:24). None of us can be talked into Easter faith, yet it does have a communal nature—we accompany one another to Easter, but no one else can say "I have seen the Lord" for us.

As Cleopas and his companion walk, they talk of all the things that had happened. Their conversation is honest and poignant—and echoes the despondency felt by the disciples after the crucifixion. Soon a stranger joins them, and the conversation deepens. In a phrase that speaks of the despair of the ages, the two disciples tell the stranger that they "had hoped" (Lk 24:21). They had hoped Jesus would be the one who would redeem Israel—redeem in the sense of political victory. But their hopes had not been his hopes. They had not yet understood what his coming had been about. The narrative tells us that this kind of hoping is over, finished. Redemption is not found in political conquests, even those that benefit one's people. Placing hope in military triumph and religious domination of one group over another does not usher in the reign of God. Cleopas and his companion were right to surrender this kind of hope, to exchange it for hope of a different kind. In a radical departure from hundreds of years of messianic expectation focused on a savior who would deliver one final blow to their enemies, theirs would become hope in a God of peace. But, as with most conversions, it would take time for it to make its way up from the depths to the surface of their consciousness.

The stranger surprises them with his insight and learning as he explains everything to them. But even a post-Easter homily delivered in person by the risen Lord does not elicit faith in the traveling disciples. They are stuck in old beliefs and weighed down by expectations not easily relinquished. Luke's narrative maintains the suspense: Even those who walk and talk with the risen One might not truly see him. Expectations can get in the way of faith. Something is burning inside of them, but the way is not yet clear. If their slow journey to faith sounds familiar, it is because the Emmaus journey belongs to each of us. I have expectations of how God's reign should come about, what fits with discipleship and what is foreign to it. I become discouraged when it seems to take too long for the all-inclusive way of compassion to become more visible in our communities of faith and in our world. Like the disciples going to Emmaus, I had been hoping . . .

As they approach the village to which they are going, the stranger walks ahead, as if to go on (Lk 24:28).

But the disciples urged him strongly, saying,
"Stay [meno] with us,
because it is almost evening and the day is now nearly over."
So he went in to stay [meno] with them. (Lk 24:29)

Stay with us. It is getting late. It is an ordinary offer of hospitality common in the Jewish world of the time. So he stays. They share a meal. It is then that this mystical journey takes on a new dimension. It begins with startling reminiscence, a remarkably keen recall—was he really a stranger? Or had they met him before? They remember that their hearts had burned within them as they walked along the road with him. He had enkindled something inside of them with his words, and his presence felt like fire. The tired hope of their forbearers, a hope dipped in blood, was giving way to Easter hope, hope that breaks bread with strangers rather than killing them.

Whatever the disciples experienced on their journey to Emmaus, it was powerful enough to cause them to return to Jerusalem, to return to their earlier path with new conviction. It was after fleeing, after giving up on their commitment, that "they sensed themselves accompanied by Jesus."[4] The holy came to them when their fervor was at its lowest ebb. In the midst of their discouragement they came face to face with a love they had not known in quite the same way before. It came to stay with them, and they had to tell the story.

The Greek word *meno* ("stay") offers an image of what these early seekers experienced. Most commonly translated "abide" or "remain," it is often used in scripture to describe inner presence—remaining united to someone even when the person is physically absent. In John's gospel the word appears several times in the priestly prayer of Christ to emphasize Jesus' continuous indwelling presence:

"Abide [meno] *in me as I abide in you." (Jn 15:4)*

"If you abide [meno] *in me,
and my words abide* [meno] *in you . . ." (Jn 15:7)*

"You will abide [meno] *in my love." (Jn 15:10)*

Stay with us. Abide in me. Remain in my love. This kind of
staying happens on the inside. The disciples on the way to
Emmaus extend an invitation to their house, but Jesus takes up
residence in their hearts. During an Emmaus journey the holy
comes to stay in a new way—a way that is not confined by structures or limited by dates on a calendar. Biblical staying has permanence. To stay with someone in this sense is to let your soul
abide with the soul of another. Long after the visit ends, the presence remains. It happens among best friends, soul mates, and
spouses who remain in one another's hearts even when physically
apart. It occurs with mothers and fathers whose children are carried in quiet awareness while they go their separate ways throughout the day. And in the most mysterious way of all, it takes place
when we meet strangers on our journey who walk with us and set
our hearts on fire before they take their leave. They are Emmaus
people who help us remember the paschal mystery by composing its story in our hearts.

For the Easter characters it is not physical proof of resurrection that becomes the final movement of the journey. Those who
visit the tomb and find it empty come away perplexed, terrified,
or amazed, but they rarely return home believers. A surprise
breakfast of grilled fish on the beach with the resurrected Jesus
does not move the disciples to faith. The companions on the way
to Emmaus meet the risen One, walk and talk with him for miles,
and still don't arrive at Easter faith—until they break bread with
him in their home.

Scholars have suggested that the Emmaus journey has the
markings of an early Christian liturgy: The disciples gather. They
listen to a recounting of the great stories. They bless, break,
and share bread. With their faith confirmed they set out again to

proclaim that the Lord has risen and remains with them. And always, the stranger among them is invited to the table.

THE MYSTERY WITHIN THE PASCHAL MYSTERY

Any serious reflection on the paschal mystery transports us into the terrain of archetype and myth. Some have likened it to the journey of the hero that is woven deeply into the human unconscious. Reflected in music and dreams, art and literature, living and dying, the paschal mystery connects to a core of veiled truth that resonates with human experience from antiquity and continues to bubble up from the unconscious in every age. Like a symphony, the great myths have an overture introducing the music, a heroic struggle, a sense of demise, a resilient breakthrough, and a quiet reprise. The paschal mystery also reenacts the vision quest, wherein the searcher sets out on a journey, confronts dark forces, is initiated into the toil of life, is profoundly wounded by the adventure, but somehow emerges triumphant. This simply means that Jesus walked the path that human beings walk as we engage life, wrestle with evil, develop wisdom and courage, and end our journey, hopefully inspiring others along the way to accomplish the same feat.

Like any great symphony, vision quest, or archetypal journey, the paschal mystery is meant to be fully engaged, entered into in its entirety, and not disassembled. Crucifixion, death, ascension, and resurrection each has its individual emotional nuance. But feeling the music of one without its accompanying movements is incomplete. Although it can be tempting to seek only resurrection and leave the cross behind, few of us are offered a lifetime of Easter energy that excludes all hints of pain. This is central to the mystery—the embrace of the cross is the only way to Easter.

A less common enticement, but nonetheless real for some, is the reverse: settling for suffering when joy is an option. Some among us find it strangely rewarding to be miserable. We would rather stay locked in hurt, grief, and various debilitations than give up resentments, self-pity, or the compulsions that justify our alienation from others. Herein lies another truth about the paschal mystery: not all suffering is redemptive. When I construct my own crosses and become comfortable hanging on them, I am not following in the footsteps of the one whose death was not self-imposed. Immersion in the paschal mystery implies openness to Easter even as my wounds still throb.

The paschal journey belongs to each of us. Its footsteps are traced in our lives as we negotiate the physical, psychological, and spiritual challenges inherent in human development. We are born as the overture of our unique DNA strums its notes in every cell of our bodies. Learning to coordinate our movements and to communicate with others offers us a lifetime of struggle and triumph. Somewhere in the process our hearts get broken at least once and gardens like Gethsemane open their gates to us. We will choose to engage some challenges, and others will come to us without invitation. We will be pummeled and graced, hurt and healed, holding both the inevitability of crucifixion and the possibility of resurrection together as best we can. In a final reprise we will gather up our wounds and achievements and, like Paul of Tarsus, race (or limp) to the finish line that is our life. What now? Does an empty tomb await me? Has the holy become a little more incarnate because I have lived? Will someone in a garden call my name?

DYING AND RISING EVERY DAY

The paschal mystery is a subterranean river running through our lives. Its multilayered movements are visible as we encounter obstacles and opportunities, feel the sting of failure and the delight of accomplishment. The story of the man at the pool of Beth-zatha offers an image of rising in the context of living:

> Now in Jerusalem by the Sheep Gate there is a pool, called in Hebrew Beth-zatha, which has five porticoes. In these lay many invalids—blind, lame, and paralyzed. One man was there who had been ill for thirty-eight years. When Jesus saw him lying

*there and knew that he had been there a long time, he said to
him, "Do you want to be healed?" (Jn 5:2–6)*

To someone suffering for thirty-eight years, it must have
seemed like a strange question. After all, the man had been trying. He had gone to a pool, which popular lore associated with
healing, searching to have his health restored. He had waited
there for "a long time," remaining even when his efforts met with
repeated disappointment. What does this man's story have to do
with resurrection? How does his struggle to walk again illuminate a discussion on the paschal mystery?

The man at the pool is seeking to rise, to have his life restored. His cross is the slow death of one whose life has been
paralyzed along with his legs. Confined to a sleeping mat, he is
symbolic of any one of us who can't move—who are dependent
on drugs or alcohol, trapped by destructive patterns of behavior,
or simply stuck in our growth toward wholeness. The man at the
pool is seeking release from a life of paralysis. He is trying to
heal his crippled spirit, to "get up," to move about with greater
autonomy and renewed commitment to life. Like the single father on welfare, crippled by joblessness, he is seeking resurrection one day at a time as he struggles to get to the pool of opportunity.

The Greek *anastasis* means "resurrection," and its use in scripture refers specifically to rising from the dead. In the gospels it is
the word most often used to discuss or debate the resurrection as
an event.[5] In the Easter narratives, however, some form of the
Greek *egeiro* ("raise"), or *anistemi* ("raise up" or "rise") is used
more frequently to refer to the resurrection of Jesus. Both of
these words have other usages. When the man at the pool of
Beth-zatha tells Jesus that he cannot get to the healing pool, Jesus
tells him to "rise up [*egeiro*], take your mat and walk" (Jn 5:8).
Sometimes translated "stand up" or "get up," this Greek word is
the same one that is used several times in the Easter narratives to
announce the resurrection of Jesus: "He has been raised [*egeiro*],
he is not here" (Mk 16:6). We can experience the energy of resurrection long before our physical death. Like the man at the

pool who rose up to meet his life again, anytime I rise to engage life more fully I am participating in resurrection energy.

In this sense resurrection means to embrace the challenges that call us out of ourselves, to come forward with compassion, to speak up with courage, and to stand up for justice. Resurrection energy is available to us wherever we share stories of faith and feel our hearts burning within us. We draw from its deep well when we summon up the inner strength to remove stones that curtail the human spirit and take away the obstacles standing in the way of the freedoms of the sons and daughters of God. Resurrection is about leaving behind all the inhospitable places where our life is slowly choked. Whenever we choose to move out of the tombs where it is easier to hide than change, we proclaim resurrection.

Dying and rising seem to go together. Little deaths and larger ones, even those horrific encounters with massive loss of life, can open up the possibility of resurrection. Long-term suffering can sometimes carve out a space for unexpected expansion of the heart—but agony arrives first, and Easter can seem like a lifetime away.

AWAITING RESURRECTION

In Mark's gospel, in a story within a story, we meet two women who are experiencing different forms of dying, each of them ready for resurrection energy to enter her life (Mk 5:21–43). One is a woman who has suffered hemorrhages for twelve years. The other is a little girl, twelve years old. At first glance it might seem that the number "twelve" is the only thing they have in common, aside from the fact that they are both nameless women in need of healing.

When the story opens, the little girl's father, Jairus, a leader in the synagogue, has begged Jesus to go to his daughter and lay hands on her since she is "at the point of death" (Mk 5:23). While Jesus is on his way to their home, a bleeding woman nudges her way through the crowd, touches his cloak, and is healed. She and Jesus have a brief but moving exchange. The focus quickly shifts back to the little girl. She has died, Jesus is told. Still, he proceeds to the house and announces that she is not dead, but sleeping. Then he takes the little girl by the hand and says to her, "'Talitha cum,' which means 'Little girl, get up [*egeiro*]!' And immediately the girl got up [*anistemi*]" (Mk 5:41–42).

These solitary sisters offer us two different portraits of everyday resurrection, two different ways that the paschal mystery bursts into our lives. One woman is worn down and alone, left to fend for herself. Her condition left her ritually unclean, untouchable for twelve years. Being bold and initiating is her solitary option for rising out of her debilitation and shame—she must seize the opportunity where and when she can. She contaminates everyone she touches as she shoves her way through the large crowd that has gathered. Her gutsy determination brings her to healing and to new life. She feels its energy rise up within her body (Mk 5:29). So does Jesus.

The other recipient of early Easter energy is small and helpless, dependent on receiving care in her father's house. She can only bear her condition in silent waiting. These women, so different yet so alike, represent anyone who is incapacitated, each little girl whose childhood is cut short, every little one whose spirit is drained of life.

Though their recovery is situated in the context of healing miracles, narrated to take place before the resurrection of Jesus, the energy that hints of Easter is at work. For each woman rising to health is preceded by a conscious intention to seek the holy, an act of faith more desperate than confident. The older woman is able to take this initiative herself—like the man at the pool of Beth-zatha, only perhaps more assertive than he was, she has been trying to rise out of her isolating condition for years. Internally, she is poised for resurrection. Her courage to seek out Jesus and touch his cloak is part of the faith that restores her health. She *believes* that recovery is possible. Healing has been on her mind and in her heart for years. When the time is right, the faith that looks like Easter takes a giant leap forward. Even before her flow of blood stops, something "recovers" within her, enabling her to touch again and to be touched in return.

What is remarkable here is that all the action is concentrated not on Jesus the healer, but on the woman herself: She had endured much. She had spent all she had. She had heard about Jesus. She came up behind him. She thought, she planned, she touched, she felt. She is healed. She is the one who explains to Jesus what has happened! It is the woman herself who announces her own healing. She comes forward in fear and trembling and tells him *the whole truth* (Mk 5:33). This woman's story gives courage to any of us who exhaust our resources pursuing healing. In the end, she knows what she needs to do—the primary resource for wellness is within her. When she finally realizes this, she has a direction, but the journey isn't easy.

The little girl's situation is different. Someone else has to take initiative for her, in this case, her father. She is unable to act in her own behalf. At times we are left so weakened that all of our resources are spent coping. At other times our power has been so diminished there seems no path available to reclaim it.

Little girl, get up! Woman, stand up! Claim the power that is within you. The command extends Easter hope. In it, Jesus addresses all people who have become little, withdrawn, whose sense of self has gone to sleep. Healing power is offered to all women who do not speak or act on their own, to all men who have lost their way. Is this a story about rising from death or climbing up out of oppression? Does it speak of ancient blood taboos or modern-day depression, physical demise, or emotional death?

A shunned woman and a little girl who looked dead—she is risen! It is a long narrative of empowerment, a message of encouragement. "Give her something to eat," Jesus says (Mk 5:43), nourish her rising, feed her growth. The story is a plunge into the paschal mystery. When Easter energy is present, women come out of isolation, and little girls go to the table.

Chapter 10

Pentecost

Becoming the Holy

When the day of Pentecost had come,
they were all together in one place.
And suddenly from heaven there came a sound
like the rush of a violent wind,
and it filled the entire house where they were sitting.
Divided tongues, as of fire, appeared among them,
and a tongue rested on each of them.
All of them were filled with the Holy Spirit
and began to speak in other languages,
as the Spirit gave them ability. (Acts 2:1–4)

When it was evening on that day,
the first day of the week,
and the doors of the house where the disciples had met
were locked for fear,
Jesus came and stood among them and said,
"Peace be with you." . . .
"As the Father has sent me, so I send you."
When he had said this,
he breathed on them and said to them,
"Receive the Holy Spirit.
If you forgive the sins of any, they are forgiven them;
if you retain the sins of any, they are retained." (Jn 20:19, 21–23)

Imagine such empowerment! Wouldn't it be amazing if you were suddenly able to speak your heart and be understood by everyone—and if you understood them as well! As swift as a gust of wind, enemies would become friends, families would be united, and global tensions would give way to mutual cooperation. And there is more: What a holy power would fill the world if we actually began to forgive the sins of others, and they forgave ours. It seems too good to be true. Yet, this is the central message of the power of Pentecost.

Consistent with their individual styles, the evangelists remember this Spirit-led empowerment to carry on the mission of Jesus differently. But the details matter less than the fact that at various points in time, through experiences that differed, those who had been disciples of Jesus felt encouraged by a deeply felt presence that they could only call the spirit of the holy. It consumed them like fire, rushing through them with new eagerness, a passion unlike anything they had ever known. Once again, a dramatic story could help convey the truth of it.

PENTECOST: METAPHOR FOR EMPOWERMENT

The rare word *pentecost* ("fiftieth") is a reference to the feast of weeks, an Israelite-Jewish festival celebrating the firstfruits of the grain harvest (Ex 23:14–17; 34:22).[1] Scholars have different opinions about how this agricultural festival came to be associated with the Pentecost event described in Acts 2. The word itself *(pentecost)* does not shed light on the relationship, other than to suggest that early disciples may have participated in a Pentecost pilgrimage festival, and Luke chose that event as the setting to narrate the Spirit-driven enthusiasm remembered of the early church.[2] The Lucan Pentecost narrative fits the category of a story of faith—another *imaginative retelling* intended to dramatize the charismatic zeal present in the early church. "Pentecost presses the question of the historical foundation of these episodes since neither the miracle of the tongues nor the chronological distance of the outpouring of the Spirit from Easter (cf.

John 20:22!) is supported by any other NT author."[3] All the evangelists except Luke connect Spirit-enhanced empowerment for the future mission to the ascension-resurrection events. But the setting is less significant than the fact that the disciples experienced holy authority to act as Jesus had acted. Luke reports that their speech was the very first manifestation of the Spirit's effect: when they spoke those who heard *understood!*

In Mark, the eleven are commissioned to "proclaim the good news to the whole creation," and Jesus is then "taken up into heaven" immediately after speaking to them (Mk 16:15, 19).[4] Matthew's Jesus first confers power on Peter (Mt 16:19), then extends the authority to "bind and loose" to all of the ministers (Mt 18:18). After the death-resurrection events, the eleven are commissioned to make disciples of all nations and baptize, and Jesus promises to be with them always, but no formal sending of the Spirit or ascension is described (Mt 28:19–20). John's gospel includes a recognized sending of the Spirit when Jesus breathes on the fearful disciples (minus Thomas) who are locked in the house (Jn 20:22–23). Setting up his Pentecost experience in Acts 2, Luke alone tells his followers to "stay here in the city until you have been clothed with power from on high" (Lk 24:49). Jesus then blesses them and ascends (Lk 24:50–51). It appears that the spirit of God had a variety of options for empowering in the early church! The same is true today.

How personally should any of us take a commission to forgive sins, proclaim the good news, and baptize? How personally do you take it? When was the last time that you said the words, "I forgive you"? A friend hurts my feelings and says she is sorry. A co-worker apologizes for slacking off, leaving me with more than my share of work. My partner is unusually irritable, and I know it is because she is tired. My husband forgets my birthday. Do I offer genuine forgiveness, or do I hold a grudge? Do I tap into the Pentecost authority within me and release my anger, or do I continue to nurse it, finding little ways to punish others for offending me? Binding and loosing is a power conferred on disciples, both yesterday and today. Extending words of forgiveness is Pentecost behavior, one that flows from having drawn in the breath of the Spirit. The narrative of Pentecost in Acts 2 lives on each time my words promote understanding, every time my forgiveness is genuine, each day that my way of being with people makes it a little easier for them to feel included.

"Luke was not the first to tell the (Pentecost) story." He edits previous accounts in circulation at the time, and adds detail from Israel's biblical stories to create a narrative about what began as an "initial explosion of faith in the risen Jesus."[5] In whatever ways the various traditions developed, the first tentative leaders of a small sect within Judaism that would one day become a church gradually moved from terror and hiding to speaking out boldly about Jesus of Nazareth. His vision became their vision. His life of teaching and healing became theirs as the formerly stumbling and confused disciples emerge as apostles who are full of a spirit that cannot be contained. This ought to serve as encouragement for those of us today who often feel more like the stumbling and confused disciples that Jesus first knew. Becoming full of the spirit of holiness is our destiny as Christians.

TOGETHER IN ONE PLACE

Have you ever been "together in one place" with a group of others and felt alone? The believers had assembled in one physical location, but they were only a diverse group of women and men, variously identified as disciples, relatives, and friends of Jesus, numbering about a hundred and twenty people (Acts 1:12–16). Mentioned for the last time in the Christian writings, Mary, the mother of Jesus is said to be among them.

Prior to the Pentecost event, this young community of believers is presented as a somewhat hapless band, devoted to prayer, but still wondering when Jesus will restore the kingdom to Israel (Acts 1:6, 13–14). Immediately after Luke reports the ascension of Jesus, some of these bewildered believers do not seem to know what to do next, except stare heavenward:

"Men of Galilee, why do you stand looking up toward heaven?
This Jesus, who has been taken up from you into heaven,

will come in the same way
as you saw him go into heaven." (Acts 1:11)

It is a rather unflattering depiction, designed less to show the eagerness of those assembled to see Jesus again than to emphasize the community's need for the power of the Spirit. The question echoes that put to the women at the empty tomb: "Why do you look for the living among the dead?" (Lk 24:5). Luke's penchant for posing questions that are as timeless as they are challenging is masterful. Perplexity that leads to immobilization, for Luke, leads nowhere. Then, as now, gazing into space is a helpless response to confusion. Seeking life in empty places only prolongs debilitation.

Luke's questions are addressed not only to mesmerized and traumatized disciples of his day, but to any of us jolted by circumstances that have left us feeling stuck, dazed, and without a clue what to do to move forward: I feel trapped in a loveless marriage and my spouse won't talk about it. My job is so draining that I dread going to work, but I need the salary. Depression seems to have crept into my life like a gray cloud, but I can't afford counseling. Since my wife died, I hardly know what to do with myself when I come home from work. I wonder why my grown children don't seem to come around anymore but I am afraid to stir things up by raising the question with them. Like the early followers of Jesus, we can become caught, bereft of solutions to the baffling situations in which we find ourselves. We can easily respond with the helplessness of the early disciples— plant ourselves into the ground and stare at the sky, or alternatively, look for life in self-defeating behaviors.

After the Pentecost experience this group of early followers is identified in a new way—instead of staring at clouds the disciples are speaking to people, and doing so with uncharacteristic confidence. More important, they are transformed from being "together" in "one place [*homou*]" to being together in "one mind [*homothymadon*]." A genuine experience of Pentecost creates community. As newly strengthened believers, their physical proximity deepens into genuine unity of mind and heart:

All who believed were together [homothymadon]
and had all things in common. *(Acts 2:44)*

Although most certainly an idealized description, Acts 2 (and
Acts 4:32–34) remembers an early group of believers characterized by deep bonds of harmony as a result of the outpouring of
the Holy Spirit. Transformed from a stunned group to decisive,
unified ministers filled with a newfound confidence in the message they are to preach, the women and men of Pentecost carry
forward the reign of God in the physical absence of Jesus.
Through the Spirit, Jesus has truly come to abide with them in a
new way.

Together in one place—how does this pre-Pentecost image speak
to us today? Staying in the same house, traveling with the same
group of people, even praying together does not, in itself, point
to the presence of an Easter community. Upper rooms might
offer safety in numbers, but as any of us who have shared a house
with others know so well, physical nearness is not synonymous
with *homothymadon*—being of one mind and one heart. Even being married does not necessarily announce Easter unity. Staring
up into the sky in unison is not an inevitable precursor to Pentecost. The early believers needed a new "river experience," a baptism that would empower them with spirit and fire. Most of us
require the same radical plunge, often again and again, if Pentecost passion is to remain alive in us and in our relationships. Some
people call it conversion, others, renewal. Luke called it Pentecost.

BEING ONE HEART

Being of one heart and one mind refers to inner connectedness,
not identical thinking and feeling. This kind of complete inter-
penetration of spirit is particularly emphasized in the Johannine
writings to describe the union between Jesus and Abba, as well as
the quality of relationship that Jesus prayed would characterize
his disciples: "Abba and I are one" (Jn 10:30).

When Jesus speaks of his oneness with Abba, he is not obliterating the difference between them. He is describing an intimate bond, a oneness of being whereby the individuality of each is preserved while mutual access provides a connection that cannot be severed. In a long and poetic priestly prayer, Jesus asks that both his disciples and those who hear their message will come to experience this same kind of reciprocal love:

> *"The glory* [doxa] *that you have given me*
> *I have given them,*
> *so that they may be one as we are one." (Jn 17:22)*

> *"I in them and you in me,*
> *that they may become completely one." (Jn 17:23)*

His words tender, as befits their closeness, Jesus talks to the one with whom he has experienced total union. He says that he has been given *glory*, and that this is the foundation of his oneness with Abba, and he has, in return, given *glory* to those he has come to love. What does this really mean? The Greek *doxa* ("glory" or "splendor") does not adequately convey the notion as well as its Hebrew original, *kabod (kavod)* ("weight" or "heaviness"). Jesus feels that he has been enveloped by the *weight* of Abba, filled by the *heaviness* of the holy. The fullness of God has infiltrated his being, leaving him soaked in love. It has permeated the air he breathes, broken into the thoughts he thinks, affected the spontaneous feelings he experiences. This *kavod* has created such fullness in his being that it spills out of him. He can only hope to pass it on to all those he loves, and to those that they love in turn. He knows they will need the presence of an advocate (spirit) as they meet this love in their lives and try to share it with responsibility and compassion.

The first description of the early community of believers after the Pentecost experience of Acts employs the same image of oneness for which Jesus prays in John's gospel. Although Luke-Acts predates the gospel of John, there is a shared conviction (inspiration) among biblical writers that the followers of Jesus ought to be recognized by their oneness of mind and heart. Paul, who is the first to write after the crucifixion-resurrection events, repeatedly pleads for such union among the followers of Jesus. In a perceptive and moving reflection on biblical oneness, Paul uses the image of the human body to illustrate the unity that should characterize the members of the Christian community:

> *For just as the body is one and has many members,*
> *and all the members of the body,*
> *though many, are one body, so it is with Christ.*
> *For in the one Spirit we were all baptized*
> *into one body. (1 Cor 12:12–13)*

In addition to his emphasis on unity, Paul recognizes that like the distinctive parts of the physical body, each member within the one body of Christ is *unique*—having different functions, yet remaining interconnected—one in spirit. Like oxygen-rich blood in the body, the Spirit of the holy nourishes every member of the community. Paul understands that the oneness flowing from baptism is a Spirit-inspired unity that presupposes diversity. While Paul's understanding of this is contingent upon the particularities unique to the early foundations of Christianity, his endorsement of the concept of diversity within unity is clear. Believers can "drink of one Spirit" (1 Cor 12:13) and still maintain their individuality.

You and I can have different political persuasions but still care deeply about each other. Liberal and conservative might identify our diverse religious views, but need not diminish our genuine care for one another. I can disagree adamantly with you and also treat you with respect. Still, it is always challenging to allow love to be the larger influence in our lives when we don't agree on significant values. Have you ever known families that have adopted the practice of avoiding any mention of religion or politics at their gathering lest the discussion turn volatile? Paul's plea to the Christians at Corinth is in itself a testimony to how difficult achieving and maintaining Christian unity is for early believers. It seems no different for us.

Although the post-Pentecost community in the Acts of the Apostles is described as tight-knit and generous, other Christian accounts identify groups sharply divided by differing ideologies. It appears that the intensity of Spirit-empowered commitment in the early church was vulnerable to the same disruptive conflicts seen today among those who profess belief in Christianity. Such discord often has less to do with the basic tenets of early Christian faith—that Jesus of Nazareth lived, was crucified, and is now risen—than with internal politics related to belonging and inclusivity. Central among them was the issue of circumcision: Do Gentile converts to Christianity have to become circumcised and follow the Jewish dietary laws in order to be baptized? Do Gentiles have to become like Jews to be welcome in the community of believers? Put another way, does everyone have to be exactly alike in order to belong?

Although it might seem that dietary regulations and circumcision are antiquated issues for religious debate, they are still around today in altered form: Can homosexual persons have their unions blessed in ceremonies similar to marriage? Should they be ordained? Can women fully represent Christ? Should the Catholic Church ordain women? Does everyone have to find salvation through Jesus? Can Muslims and Buddhists experience fullness of religious faith? How much diversity of thought and practice can a community invite? Paul, of course, was adamant that physical characteristics and individual differences of background should not be the determining criteria for baptism—the ultimate rite of acceptance into the community. For Paul, the spirit of the law is always superior to the letter of the law. What is inside the core being of the seeker is more important than what is cut into the flesh—or carved into the heart. If love is the most important issue, as Jesus repeatedly said it was, why are we even asking such questions?

BLOGGING FOR CHRIST

Modern times have witnessed increasing discord among Christians, who sometimes bear little resemblance to the peaceful community gathered together after Pentecost. Being of one mind and heart is often distorted to mean absolute assent to church doctrines and unanimity of thought among those who identify as members of a believing community. This has become especially true among more reactionary Roman Catholics and some fundamentalist Christians who can tolerate nothing less than complete agreement with their particular view of what it means to be Christian or Catholic. This is seen today in Christian (so-called) radio and television talk shows and blogging sites, many of which seem increasingly dominated by rude individuals who appear entrenched in their belief that their views are the only correct ones. Often an amalgamation of religious and political banter, correcting (or attacking) others replaces honest and respectful dialogue. Talk-show hosts and telephone callers alike insult those whose views differ from theirs, and many otherwise reputable blog sites must remind participants to "keep the conversation civil"—a sad commentary on just how seriously Christians have internalized the biblical command to love one another. As noted author Karen Armstrong stated on a recent television broadcast, for some people being *right* has replaced being *compassionate* as a sign of religious commitment—a notion that Jesus of Nazareth would not recognize.

The centrality of what it means to be Christian is threatened when mean-spirited slurs and cruel accusations are hurled against anyone who expresses an opposing viewpoint. One of the greatest threats to Christianity today is not diversity of opinion but self-righteous and arrogant rejection of the very concept of diversity. Any time someone whose sincere expression of belief is met with ridicule, verbal abuse, and even violent threat, the body of Christ has suffered a wound. Nowhere in the Christian writings is there any suggestion that such destructive behavior flows from the same Spirit that swept through the house with the fire of love described in the Pentecost experience—a love that reached out equally to all.

When difference of opinion occurs, as it normally will when thinking, feeling adults honor and give voice to their varying life experiences, what might motivate the response among a community of believers? How ought people of Pentecost approach one another, especially at times of disagreement? Paul gives poetic voice to the vision that he thought essential in shaping and guiding the earliest Christian communities:

Love is patient; love is kind;
love is not envious or boastful or arrogant or rude.
It does not insist on its own way;
it is not irritable or resentful;
it does not rejoice in wrongdoing, but rejoices in the truth.
It bears all things, believes all things,
hopes all things, endures all things.
Love never ends. (1 Cor 12:4–8)

Paul's hymn to love is not intended to be an ode to sentimental idealism, but an invitation, if not a mandate, guiding Christians in their treatment of one another. Though the gospels as we know them had not yet been written when Paul writes, the earliest communities remember how Jesus singles out love as the central sign of discipleship. Here, Paul personifies love, giving each of its manifestations an identity corresponding to a virtue that was being neglected in the Corinthian community. He reminds the Christians at Corinth that the impatience and unkindness being displayed in the community are not loving (1 Cor 8:1–13), nor are envy, rudeness, and resentment.[6] For Paul, for whom the spirit is of primary importance, the believers must continually measure their behavior toward one another against the actions that are characteristic of the Spirit of holiness. Of these, love is primary. Paul does not hesitate to correct those who violate this basic Christian mandate. While he is a champion of diversity, some things are not negotiable. Being unkind, arrogant, rude, boastful, and controlling are not options in a community that is being led by the Spirit of holiness. I cannot demean other people whose opinions and values differ from mine, and still qualify as Christian. It is about as simple as that when it comes to being a Christian disciple.

TONGUES AS OF FIRE

They were on fire! But the Pentecost of the Christian writings is not a literal account of tiny flames flickering on the heads of startled apostles. It is a narrative of faith, an inner experience of the holy that becomes palpable in the early church and is initially passed on in oral stories. While the ancient origins of the Pentecost narrative are unknown, Luke is familiar with enthusiastic Spirit-directed accounts of ministry in the first communities that existed several decades before he wrote. Most certainly there was a conviction that the Spirit of holiness enlivened those first ministers, prompting bold preaching and healing actions in Jesus' name. As stories are told and retold in successive generations, images and embellishments are added to help hearers picture the events and feel their power.

Who of us after a two-week trek atop the Pacific Crest Trail does not remember the nights colder, the stars brighter, and the howls of the wolf pack more ominous as we retell the story? Adding color, sound, excitement, and danger enlivens an already gripping narrative and makes it more memorable. When a story is worth telling, it is worth sculpting to fit the needs of the hearers. So it is with the composition of Luke's richly hued Pentecost narrative.

As he had done in composing the infancy narratives of his gospel, Luke reaches back into Jewish stories to show continuity between the old and the new:

At the blast of your nostrils
the waters piled up,
You blew with your wind,
and the sea covered them. (Ex 15:8, 10)

On the morning of the third day there was thunder and lightning,
as well as a thick cloud on the mountain,
and a blast of a trumpet so loud that
all the people who were in the camp trembled. (Ex 19:16)

Vivid, anthropomorphic language used to announce theophanous events of the past is now employed to provide confirmation of the coming of the Spirit into the church. The breath out of Yahweh's nostrils, like the "mighty wind" that parted the sea for the Israelites, now blows through the house to inaugurate the new age. As smoke and fire announce God's distant presence in the past, it now draws even closer, infusing the very being of the early disciples.

Luke admits use of symbolic language when he announces the arrival of the Holy Spirit. He speaks of a sound *like* the rush of a violent wind and divided tongues *as of* fire (Acts 2:2–3). His stunning and colorful imagery proclaims the presence of the Holy Spirit in the community—a Spirit that rushes in like the wind and fills all the disciples with a fiery capacity to speak and be understood by all, *as if* their native tongue had been divided into the languages of all who would hear them.

If he wanted to make sure that future generations would be convinced of the Spirit's coming, and commit it to memory, he was successful. Pentecost is another of the Christian stories that has been widely popularized in art, music, and even jewelry, in part because of the compelling nature of Luke's symbolism. But something else happens with Luke's dramatic narrative; as with so many other biblical stories, the metaphor becomes *literalized* as well as memorialized.

This has been especially true with the image of "divided tongues, as of fire" and the subsequent ability of all the people to understand what was being said, regardless of their native language (Acts 2:3, 6). Luke's description is clearly not one of unintelligible speech, but in fact just the opposite. Each person in the crowd "heard them speaking in the native tongue of each" (Acts 2:6). The people in Luke's multinational crowd were "bewildered" and "amazed," not because the utterances of these Spirit-empowered leaders were indecipherable, but precisely because a most astonishing degree of clarity was present (Acts 2:6–7). "It is likely that the detail of the 'division of tongues' refers to the story of Babel (Gn 11:6–9; Deut. 32:8). The nations divided since Babel are re-united by the apostolic proclamation."[7] In Lucan theology apostolic preaching will not further scatter people in confusion but rather reunite them from all the ends of the earth. While his vision often seems far from realization, Luke nonetheless depicts the birth of the church as contributing to human unity.

Spirit-enabled speaking promotes recognition and comprehension. When teaching, preaching, prayer, and other forms of communication are Spirit inspired, transparency of meaning is also present. The recipients hear and understand what is being said because care has been taken to adapt the message to meet their unique needs and backgrounds. The ambivalence in Luke's gathering crowd at such powerful exchange is understandable. So much of human speech is uttered with little thought as to its capacity to make sense, to get through to those who hear it.

It is important not to fuse the verbal lucidity of the Christian Pentecost described in Luke with the glossolalia (speaking in tongues) criticized by Paul (1 Cor 14:2–19). Paul was familiar, some thirty or forty years before Luke narrated the Christian Pentecost event, with the style of ecstatic utterances of some in the Corinthian community. Present in various Christian and pagan circles, glossolalia is characterized by *incomprehensible* speech or prayer that requires interpretation in order to have meaning for the community. While Paul does not condemn glossolalia, his letter to the Corinthians indicates that its use troubles him and that its expression has become problematic, owing in part to competition among those who manifest different gifts of the spirit. Paul makes it clear that speaking in tongues is not as edifying for the community as is prophesy, and he urges the Corinthians to pray for this spiritual gift (prophesy), while never forgetting that love is the highest gift of all (1 Cor 13—14). For Paul, the most significant indicator of the presence of the Holy Spirit is behavior that builds up the community. The community can do without speaking in tongues, but it cannot do without love. Emphasized in his earliest letter, Paul repeats this message often: "For you yourselves have been taught by God to love one another" (1 Thes 4:9). In one of his most pointed yet poetic admonitions, he says: "If I speak in the tongues of mortals and of angels, but do not have love, I am a noisy gong or a clanging cymbal" (1 Cor 13:1). There is little more to be said about where Paul stood with reference to the gifts of the spirit.

We all have choices between loving and unloving speech: A father calmly suggests that his children take turns talking rather than yelling at them to shut up. Instead of going to bed in silent anger a wife tells her husband that she misses him and feels lonely when he watches TV every night. A religious educator raises her concerns with her team about the work load while resisting the temptation to gossip about their laziness behind their backs. A leader of a religious congregation promotes courses in healthy communication for the members. Exchanging the noisy gong for the tongue of love takes discipline. But it is love that lasts.

PENTECOST AGAIN

Along with other Christian writings, the Acts of the Apostles announces many Pentecosts. The wind and fire ushering in the Spirit in Acts 2 may be the most dramatic, but it is not the only sending of the Spirit of holiness into the community of the world. Pentecost is a timeless event that happens each time the breath of the spirit reanimates a community with fiery passion that further commits it to advancing God's reign of justice in the world.

Pope John XXIII understood the enduring nature of Pentecost when he opened the Second Vatican Council in 1962. He saw the Holy Spirit at work in the world of his day wherever he witnessed signs of human empowerment. The emergence of developing nations, the growing rights of the working class, and women's claim to equality were vital signs of the times—markers of the work of the spirit that John highlighted in his encyclical *Pacem In Terris*. He wanted a Catholic Church that promoted greater compassion and freedom for all of God's people, a church that worked with the spirit of justice, not one that appeared to fight it with harsh rules and an expansion of orthodoxy. Beloved Pope John, as he was often called, labeled Vatican II "a new Pentecost."[8] He envisioned it as an opportunity to open the windows of a church where the air had grown stale with aging legalisms. He wanted to allow the fresh wind of the Spirit to breathe new life and passion into the church's way of engaging the world. He saw in such a council a way for the Pentecost energy of the Acts of the Apostles to be called forth again, to be another new beginning.

He saw Pentecost as an active, ongoing occurrence with noticeable consequences.

Pentecost can frighten and anger people as well as inspire and enliven them. It happened in the early church and continues to happen today. In Luke's Pentecost event, many who heard the emboldened, spirit-enhanced speech of the apostles were amazed. "Others sneered and said, 'They are filled with new wine'" (Acts 2:13). Mocking those whose message feels threatening is at least as old as the scriptures. Even as Vatican II was beginning, those whose power would be jeopardized by a new Pentecost were scrambling in the background, putting ecclesiastical gears in motion to harness the wind and blow out the fire.

Not long after Pope John XXIII's body was brought into St. Peter's Basilica in Rome, I visited there with a small group of friends. As we stood in front of the glass casket holding the remains of gentle Pope John, one of my friends whispered, "He's lost weight." At first we all smiled. We remembered John XXIII as a portly man, and now his body had all but disappeared, with only the garments that lay flat against the bottom of the casket remaining. He's lost weight. His shrunken body became a metaphor for his vision of a new Pentecost—it too had "lost weight." His robust hope for a more open and alive church had shriveled, become flat by many accounts, fallen victim to men whose hearts can seem as small as the church they are trying to control. Pentecost can ask too much sometimes. For some, an unfettered spirit, especially a holy one, needs to be reigned in lest it become accustomed to blowing where it will.

PENTECOST IN ASIA

Thirty-three years after the close of Vatican II, on April 19, 1998, an invitation was extended to Asian Synod of Bishops, which then gathered to address the issues related to the church in Asia. Like Pope John XXIII, the Asian bishops saw an opportunity for a new Pentecost. "What would the Catholic Church look like if an unyielding search for justice and harmony characterized its mission in the world?"[9] Although they had been summoned to Rome, the instinctive spirit of harmony among the Asian bishops led them to hope for an open discussion of the concerns related to the people of the countries they represented. These concerns focused on inculturation, dialogue, and service of the poor. Having come to a new vision of church among themselves, they hoped their insights would be welcome in Rome. Tom Fox, in his powerful book *Pentecost in Asia*, chronicles the experience, where, once again, the vibrancy of Spirit-prompted speaking was eventually squelched.[10] Fear and control silenced sincere pleas by the bishops for a church that would listen to the experience of the peoples in Asia. The venerable experts of Asia went home, their vision still large, but their hopes for its reception now dimmed. Pentecost in Asia, like the Pentecost of Vatican II and the Pentecost of Luke's gospel, remain beacons of hope whose time of fulfillment is still to come.

BECOMING THE HOLY

We change as Pentecost enters us. The fire of Pentecost is passion, conviction, commitment to all that represents the reign of God. Its primary sign is transforming inner fire into passion-animated speech that aspires to get through to as many people as possible. This means that Pentecost speech requires reflection, sensitivity to others, good communication skills, and clarity of motivation. Above all, Pentecost is a feast of fiery surprise, a wind-blown explosion of love that welcomes everyone.

When Peter, filled with the Holy Spirit, bursts forth in bold declaration about Jesus, both angering and threatening the religious rulers, they ask him to cease speaking and teaching in the name of Jesus (Acts 4:8–18). In a dramatic show of courage and strength, both Peter and John attest to the force of the Spirit in them: "We cannot but speak of what we have seen and heard" (Acts 4:20). When the Spirit of God has filled a person, the impetus to speak and act out of this holy energy is overpowering. Stifling the word of the holy does violence to both the message

and the messenger. Can you recall a time when you felt what
Peter and John felt—compelled to speak up, to be bold, no matter the consequences?

- A laboratory worker "blows the whistle" about falsified research for a new drug and loses his job.
- A newspaper reporter digs deeper to substantiate information about the global coverup of clergy sexual abuse and is
  accused of being anti-Catholic.
- A woman, battered one last time, finally goes to a shelter and
  reports the domestic abuse she has endured for years. Her
  husband threatens her life when he finds out.
- Catholic laypeople and clergy continue to speak their honest
  convictions in the church and world and are threatened with
  excommunication.
- With stomach in throat, a husband tells his beloved wife about
  his anger toward her.

Jeremiah understands the overpowering force of the holy and
laments the high cost of being compelled to speak of God: "O
Lord, you have enticed me, and I was enticed; you have over-
powered me, and you have prevailed. . . . If I say, 'I will not mention him, or speak any more in his name,' then within me there is
something like a burning fire shut up in my bones; I am weary
holding it in, and I cannot" (Jer 20:7–9).

Pentecost is a voice of truth that will not be stilled, even when
it is forbidden to speak. It is fire in our bones that cannot be
extinguished. Of course, not every compulsion to speak is spirit
directed, so how can I know if the passion I feel has its source in
the holy? Every person who feels like shouting out in a crowd is
not necessarily spirit directed. But there are some tests of authenticity that we can consider:

- Am I part of a healthy community of people who share my
  passion and support my voice?
- Is what I feel compelled to say consistent with gospel values
  of justice, love, and peacemaking?

- Who benefits from my vocal witness? Will anyone be damaged by it?
- Am I speaking truth to power or just venting my own anger?
- Have I consistently taken my convictions to prayer?
- Who or what is the focus of attention when I speak? Is it about me or about the reign of God?
- At the end of the day do I let go and feel peaceful?
- Am I open to being changed?

How effectively do you use your Pentecost voice? Do you let others know what you are thinking and feeling in a manner that honors their dignity? How often do you allow fear to silence your voice? Are you conscious of the basic rules of healthy communication: listen at least as much as you talk, don't monopolize the conversation or interrupt others, tell the truth, notice the emotional cues in an interaction? The more introverted among us might need to be more conscious of the importance of letting others know what we are thinking and feeling. If we are more extroverted, monitoring how often and how long we speak will be our task.

When Peter visits the house of Cornelius and baptizes his entire Gentile household, the long story reveals as much about Peter's receptivity to the ongoing energy of Pentecost as it does about the Spirit-led Gentiles assembled there (Acts 10:9—11:18). Throughout the episode Peter changes. He expands his notion of belonging and inclusivity: "I truly understand that God shows no partiality, but in every nation anyone who fears him and does what is right is acceptable to him" (Acts 10:34–35). Peter has experienced conversion! His earlier conviction about unclean and profane creatures gives way to the influence of the Spirit and he recognizes that all of God's creation is good. But an even greater surprise awaits Peter and the other circumcised believers who had accompanied him to the house of Cornelius. To the absolute astonishment of all, the Holy Spirit fell on "all who heard the word," and was poured out "even on the Gentiles" (Acts 10:44–45). Those who had been "others" for as long as Peter can remember are now part of the community. When Pentecost energy meets receptivity, holiness spreads out like an unstoppable volcanic eruption. And all who come to the table find a place card with their name on it.

ENTERING YOUR LIFE

Welcome to the feast that is your life! Your birth is announced by an angel sent by God. Your mother says yes and visits with those who understand miracles. The heavens burst forth in song when you are born. You grow in wisdom and grace as you search for your path. You are plunged into life with all its blessing and sorrow. It transforms your soul. You climb a hill and find a cross waiting for you. You die and rise time and time again. One day, when you are staring into the sky hoping for direction, you feel it: fire coming to rest on your head, burning in your bones, empowering a voice you didn't know was in you. Perhaps for the first time you speak in a manner that others understand. Yours might be words of forgiveness or encouragement. They may articulate your anger or your love. They might give voice to your convictions or your disappointments. Your words are hesitant, but they are honest. There is no violence in them. You feel power spread throughout your body as you speak. Others hear and are encouraged to find their voices. The flame burns brighter, stronger. It is Pentecost again!

Notes

Chapter 1. Christian Feasts as Metaphors

1. Raymond E. Brown, *A Coming Christ in Advent: Essays on the Gospel Narratives* (Collegeville, MN: The Liturgical Press, 1988), 9.

2. Joseph A. Fitzmyer, *Theological Studies* 25 (1964): 386–408 (contains the full Instruction and commentary).

3. In popular usage the word *myth* is sometimes used to refer to something that is not true. However, I am using the term here to mean story, legend, or tale that belongs to the literary category of mythology.

4. The first lines of the creation stories of peoples who inhabited the plains of what is now Canada and the central United States are displayed at Wanuskewin Heritage Park, a First Nations Cultural Center in Saskatoon, Saskatchewan, Canada. Archeology shows eight distinct genesis stories that predate the Genesis of the Hebrew bible by thousands of years. Images of water, earth, soil, and breath are prominent.

5. Karen Armstrong, *A Short History of Myth* (New York: Canongate Books, 2005), 4.

6. Joseph Campbell, *Myths to Live By* (New York: Viking Press, 1972), 31.

7. Armstrong, *A Short History of Myth*, 10.

8. John Dominic Crossan, *In Parables: The Challenge of the Historical Jesus* (New York: Harper and Row, 1973), 33.

9. Ibid., 32.

10. Ibid., 33.

11. Ibid., 48.

12. Gnosticism (from *gnosis*, meaning "knowledge") is a Greek philosophy that stressed secret knowledge that could be understood/known only by the elite.

Chapter 2. Annunciation

1. Collier was commissioned to create the Catholic Memorial at Ground Zero.

2. Eugene LaVerdiere, SSS, *Luke: A Biblical Theological Commentary* (Wilmington, DE: Michael Glazier, 1980).
3. Ibid., 20.
4. Elizabeth A. Johnson, *Truly Our Sister: A Theology of Mary in the Communion of Saints* (New York: Continuum International Publishing Group, 2003), 251.
5. The Hebrew word *almah*, meaning "maiden of marriageable age," was translated into a Greek word that commonly meant "virgin." The Hebrew source and its translation are discussed in many biblical commentaries.
6. Johnson, *Truly Our Sister*.
7. For an excellent summary of this, see ibid.
8. Ibid., 31–33.
9. Catharina Halkes, "Mary in My Life," in *Mary, Yesterday, Today, Tomorrow*, ed. Edward Schillebeeckx and Catharina Halkes (New York: Crossroad, 1993), 75.
10. Johnson, *Truly Our Sister*.
11. Greg Mortenson, *Stones into Schools: Promoting Peace with Books, not Bombs, in Afghanistan and Pakistan* (New York: Viking Press, 2009), 14.
12. John Ayto, *Dictionary of Word Origins* (New York: Arcade Publishing Company, 1990), 525.
13. Johnson, *Truly Our Sister*, 230.
14. Ibid.
15. Vincent G. Harding, "Our Children Are Waiting for the Music," *Sojourners Magazine* (January 2010), 35.
16. LaVerdiere, *Luke*, 20.
17. Johnson, *Truly Our Sister*, 253.

Chapter 3. Visitation

1. Elizabeth A. Johnson, *Truly Our Sister: A Theology of Mary in the Communion of Saints* (New York: Continuum International Publishing Group, 2003), 259.
2. Rebecca, a college student at a West Coast University in the Pacific Northwest (2010).
3. Raymond E. Brown, *An Introduction to the New Testament* (New York: Doubleday Publishing, 1997), 232.
4. Ibid.
5. Johnson, *Truly Our Sister*, 260.
6. Robert J. Karris, OFM, "The Gospel according to Luke," in *The New Jerome Biblical Commentary*, ed. Raymond E. Brown, Joseph A. Fitzmyer, and Roland E. Murphy (Englewood Cliffs, NJ: Prentice Hall, 1990), 681.

7. A classic biblical commentary is Brown, Fitzmyer, and Murphy, *The New Jerome Biblical Commentary*.

8. Johnson, *Truly Our Sister*.

9. Karris, "The Gospel according to Luke," 680.

10. Joel B. Green, *The Gospel of Luke* (Grand Rapids, MI: William B. Eerdmans, 1997), 80–81.

11. Eugene LaVerdiere, SSS, *Luke: A Biblical Theological Commentary* (Wilmington, DE: Michael Glazier, 1980), 20. Here, I am including Elizabeth in LaVerdiere's observation that readers identify with Mary, allowing her story to become their story.

12. Elisabeth Schussler-Fiorenza, *In Memory of Her: A Feminist Reconstruction of Christian Origins* (New York: Crossroad, 1983).

13. Johnson, *Truly Our Sister*, 262.

14. Marina Warner, *Alone of All Her Sex: The Myth and Cult of the Virgin Mary* (New York: Random House, 1976).

15. Ibid. Although dated, the book is well researched and offers an interesting perspective on Mary's various titles.

Chapter 4. Nativity

1. John Dominic Crossan, *Jesus: A Revolutionary Biography* (San Francisco: Harper, 1994), 10.

2. Luke Timothy Johnson, *The Gospel of Luke* (Collegeville, MN: The Liturgical Press, 1991), 3.

3. Raymond E. Brown, *The Birth of the Messiah: A Commentary on the Infancy Narratives in the Gospels of Matthew and Luke* (New York: Doubleday, 1993).

4. John L. Heagle, *Justice Rising: The Emerging Biblical Vision* (Maryknoll, NY: Orbis Books, 2010).

5. Benedict T. Viviano, OP, "The Gospel according to Matthew," in *The New Jerome Biblical Commentary*, ed. Raymond E. Brown, Joseph A. Fitzmyer, and Roland E. Murphy (Englewood Cliffs, NJ: Prentice Hall, 1990), 636.

6. Jerry Bleem, OFM, "In the Eye of the Beholder," art meditation, *U.S. Catholic* (December 2007).

7. Walter Wink, *The Human Being: Jesus and the Enigma of the Son of the Man* (Minneapolis, MN: Fortress Press, 2001).

8. Ibid., 19.

9. Ibid., 200–201.

10. Raymond E. Brown, *An Introduction to the New Testament* (New York: Doubleday, 1997), 341.

Chapter 5. Baptism

1. Robert J. Karris, OFM, "The Gospel according to Luke," in *The New Jerome Biblical Commentary*, ed. Raymond E. Brown, Joseph A. Fitzmyer, and Roland E. Murphy (Englewood Cliffs, NJ: Prentice Hall, 1990), 687.

2. Carl G. Jung, *Structure and Dynamics of the Psyche*, volume 8 in *Collected Works of C. G. Jung*, ed. G. Adler and R. F. C. Hull (Princeton, NJ: Princeton University Press, 1969), 794.

3. Ibid.

4. Alice Walker, *The Color Purple* (New York: Harcourt Brace Jovanovich, 1982), 214.

5. Walter Wink, *The Human Being: Jesus and the Enigma of the Son of the Man* (Minneapolis, MN: Augsburg Fortress Press, 2002), 5.

Chapter 6. Temptation

1. Eugene LaVerdiere, SSS, *Luke: A Biblical Theological Commentary* (Wilmington, DE: Michael Glazier, 1980), 55.

2. Walter Wink, *The Human Being: Jesus and the Enigma of the Son of the Man* (Minneapolis, MN: Fortress Press, 2001), 122.

3. Benedict T. Viviano, OP, "The Gospel according to Matthew," in *The New Jerome Biblical Commentary*, ed. Raymond E. Brown, Joseph A. Fitzmyer, and Roland E. Murphy (Englewood Cliffs, NJ: Prentice Hall, 1990), 645.

4. Neil Douglas-Klotz, *Prayers of the Cosmos: Meditations on the Aramaic Words of Jesus* (New York: HarperCollins Publishers, 1990), 10.

5. Ibid.

6. Wink, *The Human Being*, 30.

7. Paul R. McReynolds, ed., *Word Study Greek-English New Testament (NRSV)* (Carol Stream, IL: Tyndale House Publishers, 1999), 185.

Chapter 7. Transfiguration

1. Benedict T. Viviano, OP, "The Gospel according to Matthew," in *The New Jerome Biblical Commentary*, ed. Raymond E. Brown, Joseph A. Fitzmyer, and Roland E. Murphy (Englewood Cliffs, NJ: Prentice Hall, 1990), 660.

2. Ibid.

3. John L. McKenzie, "Aspects of Old Testament Thought," in Brown, Fitzmyer, and Murphy, *The New Jerome Biblical Commentary*, 1286.

4. Mark S. Smith, *The Origins of Biblical Monotheism: Israel's Polytheistic Background and the Ugaritic Texts* (New York: Oxford University Press, 2001), 135.

5. David Leeming, *The Oxford Companion to World Mythology* (London: Oxford University Press, 2005), 118.

6. Van Wijk-Bos, *Reimagining God: The Case for Scriptural Diversity* (Louisville, KY: Westminster John Knox Press, 1995), 27.

7. Robert J. Karris, OFM, "The Gospel according to Luke," in Brown, Fitzmyer, and Murphy, *The New Jerome Biblical Commentary*, 689.

Chapter 8. Suffering

1. Two monographs from the early church are devoted entirely to the question of emotion in God: Lactantius's *De Ira Dei* and Gregorius Thaumaturgus's *Ad Theopompum*. See Marcel Sarot, *Does God Suffer? Ars Disputandi*, vol. 1 (Utrecht: University of Utrecht, 2002), 7.

2. J. Stevenson, ed., *Creeds, Councils and Controversies* (London: SPCK, London, 1966), 336.

3. Elizabeth A. Johnson, *Quest for the Living God: Mapping Frontiers in the Theology of God* (New York: Continuum, 2008), 56.

4. William Sloane Coffin, "Eulogy for Alex," adapted from a sermon delivered at Riverside Church, New York, ten days after his son, Alex, was killed in a car accident.

5. Johnson, *Quest for the Living God*, 49–69.

6. Johann Baptist Metz, *A Passion for God: The Mystical-Political Dimension of Christianity* (New York: Paulist Press, 1998).

7. Ibid., 158.

8. Jürgen Moltmann, *History and the Triune God: Contributions to Trinitarian Theology*. trans. John Bowden (New York: Crossroad, 1992), 29.

9. Metz, *A Passion for God*.

10. Johnson, *Quest for the Living God*, 65.

11. Stephen Finlan, *Problems with Atonement: The Origins of, and Controversy about, the Atonement Doctrine* (Collegeville, MN: The Liturgical Press, 2005).

12. Wink, *The Human Being: Jesus and the Enigma of the Son of the Man* (Minneapolis, MN: Fortress Press, 2001), 117.

13. Robert J. Karris, OFM, "The Gospel according to Luke," in *The New Jerome Biblical Commentary*, ed. Raymond E. Brown, Joseph A. Fitzmyer, and Roland E. Murphy (Englewood Cliffs, NJ: Prentice Hall, 1990), 699.

Chapter 9. Easter

1. Walter Wink, *The Human Being: Jesus and the Enigma of the Son of Man* (Minneapolis, MN: Augsburg Fortress Press, 2002), 152.

2. Elizabeth A. Johnson, *Truly Our Sister: A Theology of Mary in the Communion of Saints* (New York: Continuum International Publishing Group, 2003), 100.

3. Raymond E. Brown, *An Introduction to the New Testament* (New York: Doubleday Publishing, 1997), 360.

4. Wink, *The Human Being*, 153.

5. After the apostles had experienced the death-resurrection mysteries, the word *anastasis* is applied to the resurrection of Jesus, but almost exclusively in the Acts of the Apostles and in the Pauline writings.

Chapter 10. Pentecost

1. John L. McKenzie, SJ, *Dictionary of the Bible* (New York: Macmillan Publishing Co., 1965), 657–58.

2. Richard J. Dillon, "The Acts of the Apostles," in *The New Jerome Biblical Commentary*, ed. Raymond E. Brown, Joseph A. Fitzmyer, and Roland E. Murphy (Englewood Cliffs, NJ: Prentice Hall, 1990), 730–31.

3. Ibid., 730.

4. This commissioning is found in an extension of Mark's gospel that is not found in all the ancient manuscripts.

5. Jerome Crowe, CR, *The Acts: New Testament Message: A Biblical-Theological Commentary* (Wilmington, DE: Michael Glazier, 1979), 9.

6. Jerome Murphy-O'Connor, OP, "The First Letter to the Corinthians," in Brown, Fitzmyer, and Murphy, *The New Jerome Biblical Commentary*, 811.

7. Crowe, *The Acts*, 10–11.

8. Thomas Hughson, "Interpreting Vatican II: A New Pentecost," *Theological Studies* (March 1, 2008).

9. Thomas C. Fox, *Pentecost in Asia: A New Way of Being Church* (Maryknoll, NY: Orbis Books, 2002), front inside book jacket.

10. Ibid.